MASTERING
LAYOUT

Mike Stevens

ON THE ART OF EYE APPEAL

publications inc.

CINCINNATI, OHIO

Published by ST Publications Inc., 407 Gilbert Avenue, Cincinnati, Ohio 45202, U.S.A.

The Library of Congress has cataloged the first
    printing of this title as follows:
Stevens, Mike.
    Mastering layout : Mike Stevens on the art of eye appeal.
Cincinnati : ST Publications, c1986.
        127 p. : ill. ; 21 x 28 cm.
    Includes index.
    ISBN 0-911380-68-X

    1. Sign painting.   I . Title.
TT360.S74   1986   741.67 — dc19   85-61336
                                                      AACR 2   MARC

Library of Congress

For *Dawn Marie Stevens*

Contents

Acknowledgments

On the path to becoming a sign painter, we're exposed to many ideas and a tremendous amount of information, both on a conscious and a subconscious level. Regrettably, it is next to impossible to know or to recall the names of all the influential people in our lives. The skills and knowledge we acquire are built upon the work of our predecessors, and our character is greatly influenced by our family and friends. To posture autonomy is to deceive one's self.

I feel particularly fortunate to have been initiated into the sign business in the Oakland/San Jose/San Francisco Bay Area, at a time (1960) when there were many fine craftsmen still working. Their sense of design and quality of craftsmanship was impeccable. Many thanks to all of them. You gave positive direction to a young man's dream. The learning and business environment we start out in plays a key role in shaping our attitudes throughout our careers.

Bill Anderson and Dave Merrideth were two of the most all-around great sign painters that a young man could have had for inspiration. Al Bandara, Johnny Britto, and Ed Rose were my local showcard writer heroes. Their professional example always kept me striving to improve and respecting the art.

To the surprise of many, the art of sign painting is an intellectual pursuit. Two sign painters that played key roles in my intellectual development are Joe Barry and George Staton. Joe introduced me to the written word. George argued with me for twenty-three years. His intelligence, competitiveness, intellectual honesty and respect for life have served as an island of sanity for me.

Two contemporaries who have been a constant inspiration are Terry Wells and Harrison Todd. From my perspective, their lettering and design skills represent the "state-of-the-art."

The published works of Arthur Du Vall, Duke Wellington, Don Sturdivant, Marty Melton, and Bill Boley have influenced my work tremendously. Their creative manipulation of space and letter forms laid the groundwork for the bridge into the future for sign designers.

An artist can't succeed without the confidence and trust of his or her clientele. I am forever indebted to the many who have supported me over the years. In particular, I would like to thank Joan Gordon for her sincere friendship, referrals, and the market exposure I've received through her office; Iris Roth, for her encouragement, wit, trust, and ability to organize and communicate large orders from coast to coast; Myron Hatch, who by example demonstrated that the good guys can win. Thank you, Myron, for your inspiring integrity, and the freedom to grow while in your employ.

This book owes its success to many, but to none more so than Lynn Hollinger. Lynn's artistic and literary judgment saved this sign painter from many amateurish traps and pitfalls in writing. Without her proofreading, editing, and willingness to be a sounding board for ideas, I could not have crystallized my thinking.

I am especially grateful to Stephanie Corsbie and Carole Singleton of ST Publications for their professional guidance and editing and to Jerry Swormstedt of ST Publications for his confidence in publishing this work.

Mike Stevens
Akron, Pennsylvania
January, 1985

Foreword

This is indeed an exciting time to be in the sign business. There's a new wave of friendship and enthusiasm sweeping our trade. What was once an "every man for himself" cottage industry is now evolving into a national fraternity of progressive-thinking artists. Sign associations are springing up all around the country — sharing information and skills as never before.

It's curious how fast our thinking can change once we're exposed to good ideas...especially those we can see! You are about to have just such an experience with Mike Stevens' book — *Mastering Layout/Mike Stevens on the Art of Eye Appeal.* It crashes against the many myths and misconceptions that have plagued sign painters for generations. Mike demonstrates that we can use the same logical thinking in layout that we intuitively use in most other areas of our lives. You'll notice the marked absence of tricks, special effects, and fad styles in this book. That absence is deliberate. Tricks of the trade should be left to those whose education is yet to begin. Learning sound layout principles is best accomplished in the light of simplicity...unencumbered by embellishment that hides the real meat of the matter. Simplicity forces us to think graphically.

Our problem with layout in the past has been very similar to my disorganized hat collection. It boasts of a wide variety of styles, colors, and configurations. Some are appropriate for general wear, while others are definitely reserved for special occasions. I've got four full closets of hats to choose from every morning. When I don't see the one I want, my frustration drives me to stretch the nearest one over my skull as I rush out the door. Boy, could I use a book about organizing hat collections! A plaid flat-hat really doesn't complement a striped shirt! The one bright spot in this frustrating ritual is the joy and surprise in discovering a "long-lost" hat. At least that's what I keep telling myself.

Many of us lay out signs just about the same way I pick my hat for the day — accidentally. Success in finding a particular hat depends upon my ability to describe it to my wife ("You know, honey...the one I always wear on Wednesday"). Similarly, successful layout depends upon our ability to organize our thoughts, and to describe what we want to do. It's virtually impossible to deal with something that we can't describe or call by name. With careful study, this book will give you the answers.

Mike's skill in describing and illustrating the key elements of layout is what makes this book so very important. It is a veritable gold mine of information. The intellectual value of it will stretch your mind in a pleasurable way. The benefits to your career are beyond measure. The integrity of Mike's approach to this subject is a direct result of his deep love and respect for the sign trade. My hat collection may never get organized, but be confident, your understanding of layout will!

The last chapter, entitled "Troubleshooting Your Layout," is the crowning touch to this book. It's a checklist that enables you to systematically critique your own work. It's like having the benefit of a master craftsman go over your work with you! My immediate response was that this chapter is like a mirror. It reflects your thinking right back to you. This self-analysis will develop your powers rapidly.

There are three personal attributes you'll want to cultivate as you pursue the art and craft of sign painting — Discipline, Patience, and Concentration. Discipline is simply training ourselves to train ourselves. Patience is intelligent acceptance, and concentration is motivated devotion.

This foreword wouldn't be complete without mentioning the possibilities that lie before us as our intellectual skills develop. Cooperation between sign people is growing. The high level of communication through trade groups and associations gives evidence to this cooperation. The present is a fertile time to grow, share and be aware. Professionalism in our trade will continue to grow as we grow. The many people involved in this work deserve our support and respect. In light of this book, we stand at the threshold of new meaning and new self respect in this business.

Rick Straub
Lancaster, Pennsylvania

Introduction

All sign painters are sign designers, whether we choose to recognize it, and accept the responsibility or not. The only exception is the person who has never laid a sign out. Traditionally, the term "designer" has been limited to those who create designs for select projects, leaving the production to another department or company. This interpretation of "designer" has been a disservice to sign painters, and creates misconceptions as to the presence and value of design in all we do. Every sign reflects either good or poor design. There is no such thing as the absence of design in a sign.

As sign designers, we face the continuous challenge of adapting copy to empty space, very much like fine artists and their blank canvases. We have the same goals of communication and eye appeal. Fine sign painters are fine artists.

My purpose in writing this book is to identify and name the elements of design that are crucial to your mastery of the art of layout. I want to share information and experience with you that will take the mystery out of successful design, and encourage you to be the very best you can! Much of the material presented in this book was originally published in my monthly newsletter, *The Mike Stevens Journal.* It has been edited and elaborated upon for the sake of clarity. I promise you (beginner and old-pro alike), if you will read this book once for an overview, and then study it *thoroughly* at least two more times, your design awareness and layout capabilities will be dramatically improved. You'll be amazed at your personal growth and new sense of direction in design.

Someone once said that ninety-nine percent of the solution to a problem is 1. Correctly stating the problem, and 2. Asking the right questions. Our chief obstacles in understanding layout are the incomplete definitions of the problems, and the consequent poor quality of the questions and answers.

Sincere students of layout and lettering have had a tough time due to the anti-intellectual mystique that has surrounded the world of art in general, and sign design in particular. There is a pervasive notion that good design is the exclusive product of *naturally talented* people — born artists! The problem lies in the word "naturally." Imagine how intimidating it is for a beginning artist to hear that word. How can they master an art that is said to be natural, especially when they know in their heart of hearts that very few things have come naturally to them? Most everything they've accomplished has required study and practice (regardless of how talented other people said they were).

When we substitute the word "acquired" for the word "naturally," making it *acquired talent*, a whole new world of hope and possibility opens up for the student. They can now think in terms of learning and developing their skills without being psychologically defeated by the notion that good art is a natural talent. All good and all great sign painters acquired the skill and the knowledge through study and practice.

The unquestioned habit of attributing design success to "natural" talent has severely limited our ability to understand and communicate the basics of good design. Everyone acknowledges that some sign painters paint better-looking signs than others, and in fact, a few sign painters consistently paint better-looking signs than the industry produces as a whole. Why? Instead of the traditional dead end answer of: "Because they are more talented," ask yourself what the potential of the following answer might be. "Their signs, more often than not, look best because they are doing something graphically *right!*"

Signs either look right or they don't, just as a particular suit either looks right on you or it doesn't. It's all a matter of good and proper proportions. The ability to describe exactly why one thing looks good as opposed to another is uncommon, but the ability to choose between bad and good is quite common. When given a choice, most non-partisan people can differentiate between a quality product and an inferior alternative. Our problem in the sign industry is that we haven't accepted this reality, and unfortunately, many have even asserted the opposite. In an attempt to conceal inferior skills and mental laziness there are many who claim that the market can't tell the difference between good and bad, and if that isn't a good enough excuse for their mediocrity, they offer their favorite pseudo-intellectual bromide: "Art is subjective." They want and need to believe that there is no standard or authority that their signs can be judged by. Unfortunately, this attitude has prevailed at most levels in our industry, finding its source in a vocal minority who assert that knowledge and ability do not exist beyond their experience.

Sign painting is a skill. When developed, it is a craft and an art. To say that there is right and wrong in sign design is not to limit creativity and personal style, or to suggest that there is only one solution to a design problem. Standards of right and wrong in layout are essential to learning and communication. They are not all-inclusive answers, but rather, intellectual building blocks.

The essence of good design is revealed in the concept of symmetry as defined in the glossary. This definition is much broader than what is traditionally taught. In short, symmetry has to do with proportional relationships — the size, shape and color of things as they relate and balance with each other to form an integrated whole. Layout is an art that has scientific roots. It can be analyzed and demonstrated to be of a superior or inferior quality. The *science* is in knowing the parts and their function. The *art* is in the way they are assembled.

You can learn to be a good layout artist just as you learned simple math in grammar school. The main difference is that now you are your own disciplinarian. You must motivate and correct yourself. Just as math has its own vocabulary, so does design. You will find terms in this book that are familiar to you and others that are not. Please be patient. In this book, I describe the abstract elements and phenomena of design that are as variable yet consistent as the sunrise. If we are open and honest, we acknowledge that our perceptions are subjective and ever changing. If we have integrity and respect we acknowledge that some artists are doing something consistently right. Their signs are easily recognized because they always look good. If we have courage, we take the ego out of it and ask "Why"?

"...what we see, imagine, and conceptualize as artists is controlled to great extent by our vocabulary."

1

Natural Layout

In this book you'll be asked to harness your creative impulses and concentrate on the basic ingredients of good layout. You will learn to identify and define design components in a fresh, clear and concise manner. In this first chapter we will discuss the theories behind sign design in general, and the idea of natural layout in particular.

The key to success in design is understanding the theoretical terms of layout. It is interesting to note that what we see, imagine, and conceptualize as artists is controlled to a great extent by our vocabulary. If we don't have a name for a particular thing, chances are we will never see it. (You may want to skip to the back of the book and study the glossary of terms; understanding these words and phrases is essential in learning to "see" and understand cause and effect in all graphic imagery. At first, they may seem esoteric, but within a very short period of time they'll open up a whole new world of perception for you.)

Designing is the process of conceptualizing, of imagining what could be. We will discuss it only in terms of image appropriateness. Designing is the function of your imagination. The possibilities are limitless. What this book will provide you with are guideposts — principles of good design that will ensure the filtering out of inappropriate or weak ideas — and the layout capability to express your ideas in a professional and marketable way.

Layout is the organization and arrangement of copy, the stage when proportional relationships of positive and negative spaces are fine-tuned and adapted to a particular format. Design is the result of layout — the end effect. It is the combination and sum of all applied graphics and their relationship to the format. Think of layout as cause, and design as effect.

The solution to each layout lies in the specifications of the job, a clear understanding of design function, and a sensitivity to individual design elements and their relationship to the whole. The basic design elements are: format, positive space, negative space, line value, and color (hues, tints and tones). The function of design is to: capture the viewer's attention, inform, create a desired image, and make efficient use of materials.

From the definition of the function of design, it is possible to define *good design:* the unification and integration of individual dominant and subordinate design elements in such a way as to maximize function. Translated, that means the fulfillment of function in a tasteful and visually pleasing way.

One of the first realizations an artist must come to is that what we think or intend often controls what we consciously see. It can totally compromise our ability to perceive what actually *is*. We must have enough will, ego, and assertiveness to create, and yet, at the same time, be intellectually honest and humble enough to correct ourselves. It serves us well never to lose sight of this basic truth.

Successful layout requires a familiarity with enough alphabets and their variations to choose not only image-appropriate letter styles, but also letter forms that fit into a given format in a pleasing manner. Familiarize yourself with both upper and lower case versions, and learn to execute them in light, medium and bold line values.

To become topflight layout artists we need to develop not only the skills of a commercial artist, but also those of a copywriter and a merchandising manager. You must be able to discuss the copy with your client and edit out all unnecessary words. The goal is to simplify the copy and gain as much freedom as possible to organize and arrange it effectively. We will discuss the interpretation, arrangement and editing of copy in chapter 3.

You must assign an order of importance to the copy. Decide what the most important thought is, and give that absolute prominence. Then decide what is second most important, and so on. In no instance should one idea or message graphically compete with another. There must be a clear focal point. Organize your copy into thought groups according to subject matter and the amount of copy. When possible, form varying sizes of copy blocks. Contrasting proportions are essential to eye appeal.

Good layout leads the eye through the composition quickly by highlighting or putting emphasis on the most important information. This is achieved by varying the size and style of the letters. Establish the habit of using one dominant alphabet in conjunction with a secondary alphabet that is simple and clean. Occasionally a third alphabet may be used, but it is preferable to save this for your client's logo. To make a composition more interesting to the eye without needlessly changing alphabets, vary the line value of the letters. Think in terms of three distinct line values — light, medium and bold.

NATURAL LAYOUT

In general, you have a choice of two fundamental approaches to layout. The first is *natural layout*, which is to lay out and letter something that is visually pleasing within a given format, leaving adequate margins so that it doesn't look forced. The second approach is to do something so visually strong that it totally overpowers the format and causes it to recede as a design element. This is often referred to as a "Super Graphic." Anything between these two choices creates visual conflict with the format.

Form the habit of asking yourself at the beginning of each job which type of composition you're going to use. Lay out your sign completely before beginning to letter or paste-up your type. This will enable you to make last-minute corrections of your design. (You can be sure that you'll almost always see something to change or rearrange.)

A simple, harmonious and natural-looking layout can be one of the toughest things to create. It requires a great deal of awareness and self-restraint. To many, natural layout would seem to be more a case of *not* doing, than of doing. The artist must subordinate his imagination and creative urges to mental discipline and the sign's function and form.

THE NATURAL LAYOUT FORMULA

In order to help you begin to see new subtleties of design and harness your creative potential, I've developed a procedural formula that forces your imagination to respect the format and disciplines your skills. (See Figure 1.) This formula defines the layout area and ensures adequate margins. It protects the integrity of the format and directs you toward a natural, clean composition.

This formula will work within the proportions of most formats. Obviously, to utilize the defined areas, a minimum amount of copy is required. The idea is to compose your layout within the major silhouetted areas. The edge of the silhouette suggests the outside point of a particular line of copy. It may be necessary to exceed this point occasionally. Do not have every line of copy meet this edge. Try to develop an overall free-form type of silhouette that doesn't look too regimented or corny.

It is important to note that "A" and "B" are constants in the formula; that is to say, "A" is always equal to 15% of the *shortest* axis, and "B" is always equal to 17% of the *horizontal* axis. The axes extend from edge-of-format to edge-of-format. To take advantage of this formula, it is sometimes necessary to rearrange the order of the copy, add a word or two, or even to delete some of the copy.

In the natural layout formula diagram, there are three major areas. The large central area is reserved for the most important copy. This is the optical center of the format, established at the intersection of the vertical and horizontal axes. The two remaining areas are flexible and can be utilized as the copy and other priorities dictate.

Notice the shapes of the silhouettes created in Figure 2. They are rhythmically consistent with their formats. Get a feel for this, as this rhythm or thrust

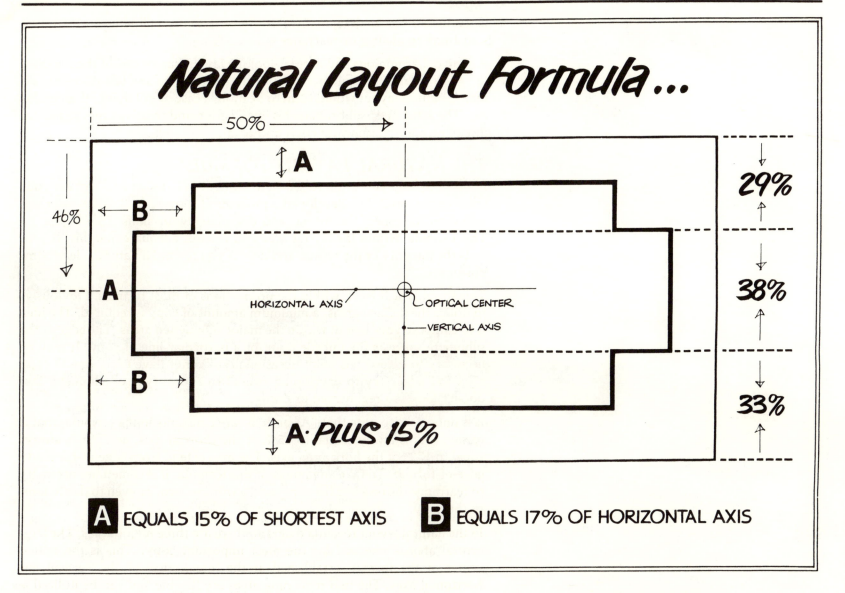

Natural Layout Formula...

50%

46%

A

29%

38%

33%

B

A

HORIZONTAL AXIS

OPTICAL CENTER

VERTICAL AXIS

B

A·PLUS 15%

A EQUALS 15% OF SHORTEST AXIS   **B** EQUALS 17% OF HORIZONTAL AXIS

Figure 1 When computing the natural layout formula, use inches as your unit of measurement. Round fractions off to the nearest half inch. A pocket calculator makes it easy.

of shape will direct you towards the most appropriate letter styles. Natural layout is dependent upon the harmonious relationship between a format and its copy blocks. The design integrity of a block of copy is maintained by correct letter and word spacing, and by the use of an alphabet that doesn't rhythmically conflict with the silhouette of the block of copy. (There are exceptions that will be discussed in later chapters.)

Study Figure 2, and notice how the shape and boundary of the silhouette change within the different format proportions.

Use natural layout as often as possible. This disciplined and simple approach will rapidly educate your eye. There is no place to hide design deficiencies. Natural layout requires that you learn to see and understand quantitative positive and negative spatial relationships. It forces you to seek theoretical layout solutions, rather than extemporaneously fill the space with something you've seen or done before.

Layout has been the most elusive skill for lettering artists. It is interesting to note that the difference between outstanding and average *lettering* artists is not nearly as great as the difference between outstanding and average *layout* artists. The difference is that lettering has always had specific guidelines: rules of proportion, spacing, and technique; clear, communicable, objective standards; and the advantage of a mental image of what the basic letter forms should look like. Whereas, the art of layout has unfortunately been treated as a mystery or a gift of birth. It isn't either one. It can be mastered by most people once they understand the parts and their relationship to the whole.

We all are trained from a very early age to see and recognize the same basic alphabet. But that's all we've been taught to see. Our intuitive, natural ability to see more has been almost completely suppressed and so we see only one element of a multi-faceted phenomenon — the positive space, or the letter. Focusing almost exclusively on the positive space is where we all begin as artists. Relatively few of us go on to retrieve and further develop our natural sensitivity to the other integral elements of design.

One of your first objectives as an artist should be to study and gain a working knowledge of *negative space*. Its value as a design element is equal to that of positive space.

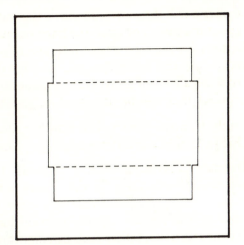

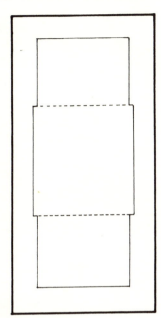

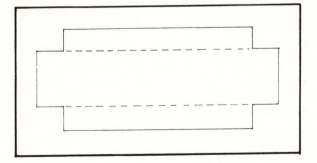

Figure 2 Notice in these sketches where the copy extends to the edge of the silhouette, and also where it is indented. Create one overall silhouette with your design, then within that shape, form sub-silhouettes of copy.

Signs can be read in two different ways. The first is *culturally*, which is to read the words, colors, and illustrations, all of which appeal to the intellect and the emotions. This type of reading is incomplete from the artist's perspective. The second way to read a sign is *graphically*, which is to read the positive and the negative spaces and their relationship to the format. A sign should make graphic as well as cultural sense. There must be a natural development of positive and negative spaces that is consistent with the order and priority of thought.

In commercial art, the primary function of negative space is to illuminate the positive. As you learn to read signs graphically and become more aware of negative space as a design element, you will be shocked to notice that most sign painters and designers actually achieve the opposite effect. Typically, they illuminate the negative space with the positive, by framing areas of negative space within the copy and between the copy and the edge of format. The result is that the background is easier to "read" than the copy.

It will take study and experience to see and control optimal proportions of positive and negative space. Some will master it more quickly than others, but eventually, all will benefit by the simple awareness of its existence.

"...it is the combination of parts, and how they relate as a whole, that determines the effectiveness and quality of a sign."

Format:
A Design Element

Format is the shape and area of the sign face, or space to design within. The format is a part of the whole. What must be understood is that it is the combination of parts, and how they relate as a whole, that determines the effectiveness and quality of a sign, not the script, cartoons, panels, color or any other one thing. The goal is to create a unified whole, whether it be a sign that is a labor of love, or a knock-out.

The format is not just a surface or an area within which artists get to do their thing, but rather a design component. Our job is to integrate the copy with the format. Take a minute sometime to look through the trade magazines. You'll notice a scarcity of signs that demonstrate an awareness of format as a design element. The majority of formats are treated as just a surface to design

Fig. 3   Fig. 4

Figure 3 The legibility of this "E" is compromised by monotony of line value, and equality of negative spaces.

Figure 4 An example of impeccable clarity. Note the strong contrast in line value, and the proportional relationships of positive and negative spaces.

on, or get off some snappy lettering on. Ignoring the format as a design element is comparable to ignoring the shape of the body you clothe.

Typical sign formats are: windows, trucks, walls and assorted paper, cardboard, wood, metal and plastic fabricated or stock pieces. The stock material signs are usually the actual format. Windows, trucks and walls sometimes represent the total format, but are often subdivided, thereby establishing an arbitrary format. In this case "arbitrary" does not mean uncontrolled by principle. Rather, it means discretionary or subject to individual judgment.

For example, in lettering a truck you may either utilize the entire vehicle or use just a portion (such as a door or rear panel), which then becomes an arbitrary format. The rightness of an arbitrary format in truck lettering is subject to the vehicle's dominant shapes and lines. For theoretical purposes, arbitrary formats will be referred to here as *sub-formats*.

Sub-formats may be created by the use of design shapes and panels, or simply by leaving enough negative space around a particular block of copy to separate it from other blocks of copy or design elements. Sub-formats are subject to the same design analysis as the dominant or major format.

SYMMETRY

Symmetry is the standard of rightness, and the goal when you are integrating the copy with the format in sign design. Not "symmetry" in the sense that you were taught in school, but rather through the eyes of a creative artist. The common definition of symmetry is "the balancing of equal parts on opposite sides of a theoretical line (axis)." This definition is incomplete, and does not address the essence of quality. Contemplate and broaden your definition of symmetry to include its philosophical base. Symmetry is the proper or due proportion of parts, and their relationship as a whole; excellence of proportion; when all individual design components are integrated so as to achieve maximum format potential. Symmetry is a wholistic concept that is based on good or tasteful relative proportions.

Figures 3 and 4 illustrate the principle of symmetry. Notice the difference in legibility of the two figures. The letter "E" in Figure 3 is totally compromised by the monotony of line value and equality of negative spaces, whereas in Figure 4 the letter is almost instantly recognizable. Note how the artist manipulated many different design elements into an integrated whole. Figure

4 is a masterful example of proper proportion of positive and negative spaces. The artist's priority of line value is impeccable!

AXES

Axes are the theoretical central lines around which an artistic form is composed or organized. The axes are used to design and integrate single or multiple graphic elements (i.e., each individual letter, shape, copy block and composition) into a symmetrical whole.

All formats have theoretical vertical and horizontal axes. Square and perfectly round formats have axes of equal length. All other formats have one axis that is longer than the other. The longer axis is known as the dominant axis.

In natural layout with a formal composition, the dominant axis dictates the general shape, thrust, rhythm, or direction of your layout. The goal is to compose your layout around the dominant axis, making it rhythmically consistent with this axis. This forms one overall silhouette that is generally framed by more negative space than it contains. The idea is to always have more negative space in the margins than within the layout. Please refer to the definition of negative space in the glossary. Think of negative space as a form of *graphic punctuation.*

Looking for silhouettes within the signs in your area and thinking in terms of graphic punctuation can be very educational. It's probably not too far from the truth to state that the harder it is to see rhythmically consistent and pleasing silhouettes within a given sign, the weaker the composition.

THE OPTICAL CENTER

In natural layout, the *optical center* of the format is found at the intersection of the vertical and horizontal axes. This is the heart of your composition. Every effort should be made to register the main copy in this area. (Refer to the natural layout formula in chapter 1 for correct placement of the axes.)

If it isn't possible to place the main copy squarely in the optical center, then the next best thing is to arrange your layout so that the silhouette containing the main copy is as proximate to the center as possible. Another possibility is to subdivide your sign with panels or design shapes, forming sub-formats.

Fig. 5

Fig. 6

The art of layout requires that we develop the ability to manipulate and modify letter forms. We must be able to expand and condense alphabets and vary their line value. In order to maintain the integrity and strength of the optical center, it is imperative that rhythms of positive and negative spaces are natural and smooth looking. Try to avoid framing pockets of negative space.

Occasionally, the main copy will not lend itself to placement in the optical center. However, before giving up, re-examine the situation. You may find that the problem is not with the copy, but with your *interpretation* of the copy. Our ability to interpret and lay out copy is controlled by two factors. The first is our cultural view, which is what we've been exposed to, what we expect to see. The second factor is our personal library of known alphabets and our ability to manipulate them. To develop beyond these factors takes time and experience. Please don't give up in frustration, for it may take a little longer to solve the old problems while you implement new ideas.

FORMAT: FOUR APPROACHES

Figure 5 is the kind of layout that inspires sign ordinances. The first question is, "Does the composition have any relationship to the format?" The answer is no, none. The only design awareness present in this sign is the subdivision of the original format.

Is there an optical center? Do the positive and negative spaces lead the eye

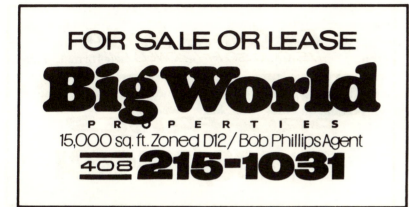

Fig. 7

Fig. 8

through the sign rhythmically and consistent with the order of thought? The answer is obviously no to both of these questions. There are many lessons that can be learned from this sign. For now, let's use it to illustrate the phenomenon of *compulsive graphic relativity.*

Compulsive graphic relativity is the phenomenon of a particular design element relating visually to the nearest dominant design counterpart. Ideally, the relation of positive spaces is consistent with the order and priority of thought. Figure 5 is rich in contradictions of thought and graphic relativity. For example, does the word "Big" relate graphically to "World," or does it relate to the edge of the sub-format? Its graphic relativity is ambiguous. Does "For Sale" relate into the composition, to the top edge of the format, or to the three zeros in 15,000? Is the negative space under and to the right of the word "Properties," the easiest design element to read on the sign?

Figure 6's composition demonstrates that even a so-called knock-out sign can and should respect the format. Note the clarity and visual impact in the optical center. The first four lines of copy read well rhythmically, but the bottom line of copy is weak. Do you see how the bottom line is broken into four separate units?

At first glance, Figure 7 is a clean-looking layout. The first two lines of copy have great clarity, but from there on it gets confusing.

Figure 8 is divided into three sub-formats. These sub-formats must be in-

Figure 5   The kind of layout that inspires sign ordinances.

Figure 6   A well-organized "knock-out" sign that follows the natural layout formula.

Figure 7   This sign would look much better if the area code had been lettered in a bold line value. Note that the composition looks weak and confusing in that area. The eye tries to read both the square footage information and the area code simultaneously.

Figure 8   Note that each panel (sub-format) is laid out as an individual sign.

tegrated with the original major format. Each sub-format or design panel should reflect the dominant rhythms of the lettering and color found in adjacent panels, to create an unified whole. For example, in Figure 8, "15,000" are tall, condensed numbers rhythmically consistent with their format. This effect is very strong, and needs a corresponding design element. "Big World" is condensed to meet that need. Rendered in black and white, this sign looks too busy, although perhaps in color it could be saved.

"Tell people immediately, without confusion, what they want to hear and need to know."

3

Copy Interpretation & Appropriate Images

Mastering the art of layout requires many different skills, some of which are obvious while others are not. Apprentices need to develop several different skills simultaneously, such as letter construction and draftsmanship, brush manipulation, using the right consistency of paint, becoming familiar with various lettering surfaces, interpreting and editing copy, layout, and who goes for the coffee. If you've been in the business for a while, you can focus more exclusively on the subject of this chapter. (You already know who goes for the coffee.)

INTERPRETING COPY

Proper interpretation and editing of copy is essential to your success as a sign designer. It is impossible to create an effective and pleasing composition without interpreting your client's copy in terms of *due graphic proportion.* Due graphic proportion is defined as the correct appropriation of space available, versus the relative importance of the copy. The skill of prioritizing copy is fairly easy to learn. Once a person is made aware of the need to do so, experience and common sense will provide most of the answers. The art lies in manipulating the volume and shape of positive and negative spaces (words, illustrations and blank space). If you misinterpret the copy or aren't able to prioritize it properly, you'll be stuck for a reasonable design solution. Creatively varying the size and shapes of words makes it possible to control spatial relationships, which is the graphic essence of design.

The term *legible* is important to discuss. It will give us a broader understanding of the goals of copy editing and interpretation, as well as another criterion for good design. To define legible simply as the ability to be read is inadequate for students of layout. It leaves out two other factors — namely, time and distance. Most signage is subject to limited viewing time and the complications of distance; i.e., the eyesight of the viewer, and the graying effect of atmospheric conditions which reduces contrast. We do not design a sign with the thought that it will be read eventually, but rather, read *now,* and if in a visually competitive environment, read first!

The term legible has a broader meaning and a few prerequisites that many artists haven't considered. In recognition of the inability of the human brain to process and understand everything it sees simultaneously, layout artists must interpret and edit copy, graphically emphasizing priority information so that the brain can discriminate immediately between important and not-so-important information. Legibility (the actual likelihood of being read) is determined more by the whole composition than by its individual parts. It is not uncommon to see signs with excruciatingly legible parts, but which, when viewed as a whole, are almost illegible due to the monotony of their proportions, and the consequent absence of a main focal point.

IDEA GROUPS

Interpreting copy involves the process of assembling it into blocks of copy or *idea groups.* An idea group may consist of a single subject or include several subjects. You'll be more successful if you keep the number of copy blocks to a minimum, and make every effort to see that they do not visually compete with each other in mass or shape. It may be necessary to add a word or two, delete or abbreviate something, or rearrange the copy in order to create symmetrical blocks. The style of lettering is determined by image appropriateness, the amount of wording versus space available, and the estimated cost of the labor in lettering. (The labor involved in different alphabets can vary tremendously. Be sure your choice of letter style is within budget.)

How do you tell which is the most important copy? Logically. All ideas and messages have a central point or issue. When verbalized, they are surrounded by accessory words — words that bridge the gap between particular subjects in speech. Ordinarily, we emphasize the subject or name of the subject, and assign varying degrees of lesser importance to the accessory words. From a design function point of view, descriptive and qualifying copy can be used to create subordinate copy blocks that flatter the main subject block.

There are many variables that can arise in editing and interpreting copy. First, there is the client, who, although completely lacking in expertise, may seek to impose his notions on the design process. You have the choice of educating him, following his dictates, compromising, or ignoring him and doing it your own way. Another situation might involve a sign that has a variety of information, all of equal importance. In this situation, you could lay out the sign as you would a food menu, only, as a menu of thoughts. Lay each subject out in distinct, but equal copy blocks. Be sure to allow more negative space between the blocks than exists anywhere within the interior of the copy blocks, but less than you have allotted for the margins of the format. To create a main focal point, label the sign with a general statement of content.

Figure 9 is an example of a sign that is so visually boring, it may be considered illegible for our purposes. Monotonous line value and mechanical rhythms of negative space render this sign virtually useless when compared to Figures 10 through 13. Figure 10 doesn't show any more imagination in interpreting the copy, but it does look professional and has its place in the market, in a library or a doctor's office, for instance. All signs do not have to be real attention-getters, but all signs should be laid out well.

To correctly interpret copy and provide your customers with the best possible value, it's important to know the purpose of a particular sign, and where

PLEASE
RING BELL
FOR
PARTS

Fig. 9

PLEASE
RING BELL
FOR
PARTS

Fig. 10

Please
Ring Bell
for
PARTS

Fig. 11

Figure 9   Monotonous line value, with crowded left- and right-hand margins.

Figure 10   Thick and thin lettering with adequate margins can save a boring composition. This layout requires that you read the entire message before understanding it.

Figure 11   This sign visually announces "Parts" before giving further instructions.

it is going to be placed. Figures 11, 12 and 13 have identical wording, but at first glance they give us different information. Each sign was designed to fulfill a different need.

Figure 11 announces "Parts" before asking you to ring the bell for service. This sign was designed to identify the location of the parts department as you approached it from down a long corridor. Figure 12 was designed to instruct people who knew they were in the parts department to ring the bell. Figure 13 was designed for people who get lost easily and have short memories.

PRIORITIZING COPY

Take a few minutes to thumb through the layout figures in this book. Study the way the copy was manipulated and graphically prioritized. Analyze the national advertisements you see on television, and in the newspapers and magazines. They are appealing to the same group of people we're painting signs for. What do they say, and how do they say it? Notice how national advertisers prioritize their printed information in comparison to the illustra-

Fig. 12

Fig. 13

tions or photographs in their ads.

Let common sense and a respect for the general public's intelligence rule the decisions you make when interpreting and editing copy. Don't repeat old traditions, such as prefacing a phone number with the words "phone" or "call," without examining their validity. (The invitation to call is implicit.)

Tell people immediately, without confusion, what they want to hear and need to know; i.e., who, what, where, when, why, and how much? The following commentary on the importance of each of these terms will give you a starting point in interpreting and editing copy. Be aware that your client's priorities and expectations for the copy may be quite different from what you might assume. If you have doubts about the relative importance of copy, seek clarification from your client.

Who   In signage, "who" is generally the name of a person, a company, or a brand. The relative importance of a name is determined by market recognition, or in the case of a rising star or a new product, the need to create

Figures 12   This sign graphically demands that you ring the bell. Note the dramatic contrast in line value, and the size of the lettering.

Figure 13   This inferior layout reads awkwardly. Note the absence of a specific focal point, and the weakness in the optical center of the sign.

market recognition. If a name is well known (a personality), it should receive prominence. A famous name, like a photograph, is worth a thousand words. It will capture the attention of all those who are interested, and encourage them to read the balance of the sign.

Brand and company names are similar to personal names in that their priority is also subject to market recognition. The difference lies in what the names are known for. A famous personality, such as a movie star or a politician, is usually widely known and is easily recognized by the market, while the market's recognition of many brand and company names is less certain due to their variety of products.

The rule of thumb is: Give absolute prominence to a name that is well known. It is the most appealing and powerful element in the copy. If a name is not so famous, it should be subordinate to the "what" (the thing, service, event, etc.). If your copy has several different well-known names, arrange them together with the "what," and give that prominence. The rationale for this is to create a single, pertinent focal point that the eye can immediately focus on.

What   The "what" in copy interpretation is second in value only to a well-known name. The "what" is the subject of the sign. It is the primary idea. If it is unclear in any way, the sign will not be read. Give prominence to the "what" by highlighting its name, or by the use of a pictorial. A good illustration is one of the most effective means of communicating. (However, a poor illustration is death to any sign, regardless of the skill in lettering and layout.)

Where   The "where" is either a simple courtesy, an essential point in the promotion (i.e., distinguishing one business or location from another), or a directional — telling people which way to go, as on a sign for use on the highway.

If a promotional sign is on-site, the "where" in the copy can be played down, unless it is, in fact, the "who" or "what." (In that case, it would be assigned prominence.) Develop a sensitivity to copy that is unnecessary or redundant. You may need to eliminate some of it, or at least have the option of playing it down in size so that you can maximize your layout.

If the "where" is at all important to a particular promotion, it still ranks second to the "who" or "what." "Where" is usually more important than date and time. If directional copy is used on a sign (e.g., turn left at next light), it is best for clarity's sake to keep it separate from the main copy area.

When   The graphic priority of date and time is determined by their context and function; that is, where and why they are announced. Most frequently, "when" is used to inform people of options and times of availability. Another use of "when" is promotional in purpose: to urge people into taking action, as in a limited time offer ("Buy Now and Save!").

If the date and time are posted simply as a courtesy or statement of availability, they should be laid out conservatively. There is little need to emphasize this information as the reader's attention has already been captured by the name or the "what." Interested parties will read well laid out copy until they've found out everything they want or need to know. Do not feel that it's necessary to keep reselling the reader graphically. Let a good thing be. It can be a fatal mistake in design to dramatically emphasize subordinate copy. More often than not, it creates a confusion and competition among the elements that can render a sign illegible.

When date and time are used to urge people into prompt action, you can start to have a little fun. Accentuate the date and time by dramatizing the alphabet. Darken the line value and increase the height of the letters or, perhaps, italicize them to create a feeling of excitement. This is one of the few times that you should think in terms of reselling the reader visually.

Why   The "why" in sign copy refers to the itemized features and benefits of the subject. This is where many sign designers go off the deep end in layout. The features and benefits of a particular product or service are always of less importance than who or what, and usually less important than when, where, and how much. However, do not make the mistake of treating features and benefits as throwaway copy either. They deserve their due. Lay them out in an orderly fashion. Your design interpretation of the subject establishes the image and character of the sign. Don't compete with it by emotionally interpreting the "why."

How Much   Generally, the only time a price should graphically dominate a sign is when the subject is already known, e.g., a price tag on a piece of merchandise. There are exceptions. For instance, many discount department stores that use "sale" type paper banners are more concerned with the atmosphere created by the signs than they are with their professionalism or legibility. Their first concern is that the appearance of a sale in progress is obvious. Their second concern is that prices are prominently displayed. Everything must look affordable.

The priority of prices in signage can be viewed in two different ways: as a matter of fact, or as a special offer. They can be the most important, or one of the least important elements on a sign. Make sure you interpret the significance of a price correctly. The traditional habit of automatically emphasizing the price needs to be checked.

In past years, graphic emphasis was placed on the words "sale" and "special" whenever a temporary price reduction was offered. These terms were considered attention-getting devices essential to the success of any promotion. Frequently, they would visually dominate the entire advertisement at the expense of the product, brand name, or store and location. (The price was usually given second billing to the words "sale" or "special.") For a variety of reasons, this approach is fading fast, and giving way to common sense and a logical set of copywriting guidelines.

The modern school of thought suggests that you can't sell something to someone unless they already want it consciously or subconsciously. Compare this with the old idea of bursting in on someone's consciousness with the words "sale" or "special" before telling them what the product or service is, and you'll begin to see the point. A part of this changeover in thinking can be attributed to the fact that most of our purchases are no longer based on need and survival, but rather for the sake of convenience and the sense of well-being they provide.

In the old days, advertisements and signs were directed at the market in general. Today, they are differentiated so as to appeal to specific socioeconomic groups of people. Many people today are comparatively well-educated, and have been exposed all their lives to goods and services awaiting their ability to purchase. With this in mind, advertisers promote the availability (what and where), benefits (need fulfillment) and value (reason to buy). They know that price is frequently a secondary consideration.

This is not to say that the prices of goods and services are not important. There are many communities and parts of the country where the economy is depressed, and people shop primarily for the most competitive prices, or, in

CONFERENCE
Directory

PRODUCT TALK
← 8 a.m. to 2 p.m. —

PLAY THEATER
← 9 a.m. to 4 p.m. —

REFRESHMENTS
Noon to 2 p.m. →

REGISTRATION
← 8 a.m to 9 a.m. —

IDENTIFICATION *Required*

Conference
DIRECTORY

◄ *PRODUCT TALK*
8 AM to 2 PM

◄ *PLAY THEATER*
9 AM to 4 PM

REFRESHMENTS ►
NOON to 2 PM

◄ *REGISTRATION*
8 AM to 9 AM

Identification
REQUIRED!

Conference
DIRECTORY

◄ PRODUCT TALK
8:00 A.M. to 2:00 P.M.

◄ PLAY THEATER
9:00 A.M. to 4:00 P.M.

► REFRESHMENTS
NOON to 2:00 P.M.

◄ REGISTRATION
8:00 A.M. to 9:00 A.M.

Identification required

Fig. 14

Fig. 15

Fig. 16

other words, they shop price before need fulfillment and quality. This segment of the market tends not to read the details of a sign until they've accepted the price. It's up to you as the designer to interpret the copy according to local expectations and conditions.

The skill of editing and interpreting copy is essential to the rational liberation of your imagination. Select alphabets on the basis of image appropriateness, and their adaptability to the available space. Your goal is to vary the size and shapes of words or groups of words to form visually pleasing copy blocks.

APPROPRIATE IMAGES

Take a look around, and you'll notice that the better layout is clean, simple, and endures over the years. Inferior layout and design is usually complicated-looking, tricky, spotty, and out of character with the subject of the sign.

Figure 14 A bulky, monotonous-looking sign.

Figure 15 This sign shows poor judgment in design. Institutional type of signage such as this should present a clean professional image as opposed to a "snappy" or cartoon look.

Figure 16 This sign is well laid out, and reflects an appropriate image.

Fig. 17

Fig. 18

Figure 17   Monotonous line value makes this sign boring to the eye.

Figure 18   Dramatic contrast gives this sign impact. The ability to correctly prioritize copy makes it possible to manipulate spaces.

The problem for most sign painters is that while their skill and dexterity with the brush improve, they remain at the first level of development in sign painting. They are in love with their craft. They are caught up emotionally with the snap and flair of certain alphabets, colors and mediums. The necessity of editing and organizing copy holds little meaning for them. To them, distinguishing between a display alphabet and a text alphabet seems like an inhibition of their spontaneity rather than a liberating and profitable realization. Instead of appropriately interpreting their client's graphic image, they indulge themselves with some experimental design that has been burning a hole in their pocket.

Good lettering is like a good sign: you don't see the personality of the sign painter — you feel the emotion of the message! Figures 14, 15 and 16 illustrate this point quite well. Figure 14 looks as if it were executed by an industrial sign painter and Figure 15 by a snappy sign painter. Figure 16 looks like a conference directory.

Figure 16 would not take as long to letter as it may appear at first. The only finished letters would be "Conference Directory." The rest of the copy (excluding the bottom line) could be a thick and thin plug letter, similar in character to optima. Notice how the hours are handled in Figure 16 as compared to Figures 14 and 15. Do you see how they help to define the silhouette of each topic, making it easier to relate one topic harmoniously to the next?

They create an overall uniform and organized appearance, which is the first thing the viewer will notice.

This is perhaps one of the least understood points. The proper relationship between symmetrical masses of positive/negative space and the format is what establishes good composition in sign design. To the degree that you are able to organize these masses and create an appropriate image, you are successful. It is within an organized layout that a professional can really begin to think in terms of speed, and take whatever shortcuts are necessary to meet the budget.

Figures 17 and 18 represent the knock-out type of banner commonly used in grocery stores. They are illustrated here to point out that no matter what kind of signs we're painting, professional standards still apply. Any fraction of extra time involved in painting Figure 18 is well worth the effort. Notice that "Ajax Cleanser" appears weak and crowded in Figure 17. In Figure 18 it totally overpowers the format, and the combination of words and price is read as a unit before the definition of the format is consciously recognized. Figure 18 illustrates the value and benefit of graphically prioritizing copy on the simplest level.

Figures 19, 20 and 21 all have the same copy, but communicate completely different company images. (The vertical lines in Figure 19 are used solely to imply a change in background color.) Which sign looks like a sign painter's emotional response to the customer's needs? Which sign is the most effective? Which sign is the most expensive, and which sign would be the fastest to paint?

Before answering these questions, let's discuss the function of real estate signs in general. Their primary function is to facilitate contact between the buyer and the seller. They advertise a particular piece of property, on site, to a specific group of people. These people already know what they are looking for and they recognize it when they see it! Therefore, the sign doesn't have to be a show stopper. The most important copy on the sign is the realtor's name or logo. Selling features and phone number are secondary, unless there are some unusual factors that distinguish the property and need to be mentioned up front. The secondary function of the sign is to familiarize the general public with the realtor's name for future business.

The author would sell Big Deal Realty the design in Figure 21. Within a short period of time the "BDR" and the panel shape would be instantly recognizable as the company's logo. It would provide a symbol for potential buyers to look for in the phone book, as there probably wouldn't be enough time for them to write down a phone number while passing in a car. Figure 21 presents a contemporary and professional image, and would not be an unnecessarily expensive sign to produce.

Figure 20 would be a little faster to paint, but doesn't have the dollar value of Figure 21. Figure 19 would be fun to paint, but is, unfortunately, an expensive and dated design. This type of design was popular in the late '40s and '50s. Figure 21 is no more contemporary or original in its individual elements than Figure 19; it just has fewer of them.

Figures 22 through 27 show the many different images that are common to showcard writing. Figure 22 was for an elegant, contemporary pub that played on an old theme. This card's design is a nice mix of old-fashioned

Fig. 19

Fig. 20

Fig. 21

Figure 19 A fun sign to paint, but the composition is dated and unnecessarily expensive.

Figure 20 A clean, inexpensive sign. Note the use of contrasting line values.

Figure 21 A contemporary sign that would give the client unique identification at a reasonable cost.

Fig. 22

Fig. 23

Fig. 24

Figure 22   Notice how the copy was prioritized in this sign.

Figure 23   A wordy, institutional sign made to look interesting.

Figure 24   Food item signs should look clean and straightforward.

alphabets, with a fresh clean look.

Figure 23 is a typical message card, appropriate for many different types of retail stores. The script was used for speed as an alternative to casual or carton lettering. Figure 24 is a typical sign for a hamburger stand, cafe, or restaurant. It is clean and straightforward. Notice that "Today's Special" was not given the kind of emphasis usually found on a card of this type. Do you think the promotion will suffer because of this?

The image Figure 24 communicates would not be appropriate for a quality hotel or restaurant. The more deluxe establishments require signs with a clean modern look and with less attention given to price.

Figure 25 is a typical trade show or hotel lobby card. This heavy copy card would be relatively fast to paint. Most trade show and convention sign orders are large, and often much of the work has heavy copy. Establish visual continuity in the signage by using consistent colors, alphabets and a

Fig. 25

Fig. 26

Fig. 27

theme border as in Figure 25. Note how small most of the copy is, and how little space is actually used for the copy. This sketch stands on its own, not because of the quality of lettering but because of its exceedingly clean composition and drama in line value.

Figure 26 would make a good "hours" poster for just about any retail store during the Christmas holidays. Once again, notice how little space is actually devoted to the lettering. This card has a feeling of quality — even in black and white. Imagine it in some modern, appropriate holiday colors. Please take special note of the fine line that joins the days and hours. This is an important design element that maintains the continuity and rhythm of each line of copy. The need for this element also arises in menu lettering. The food item should be connected to its price with a similar line or series of dots. Have you even seen a menu where the foods are in a column on the left and the prices are in a column on the right, with nothing in between but negative space? Graphically, one food item relates to the next food item instead of

Figure 25 Note the way the copy blocks are separated, yet form a unified whole.

Figure 26 Image appropriate!

Figure 27 Casual entertainment posters should look lively and fun, yet remain well-organized.

over to its corresponding price. The same thing would have happened in Figure 26 if I hadn't put the lines between the days and times. Do you see it?

Figure 27 presents an image appropriate for a country and western bar, bowling alley, or county fair — generally, any place that is informal, friendly and fun. If this were an entertainment poster for a hotel or high-class supper club, greater air space and a selection of more formal alphabets would have been necessary.

Study the figures in this chapter. Take special note of the individual image and character implicit in each sketch. The wording of a sign is only half of the story.

"Think of negative space as a form of punctuation."

Negative Space

Negative space is the area around and within letter forms, illustrations, and ornamentation, extending out to the edge of the format. It is just as important a design element as the positive space. The primary function of negative space is to illuminate the positive space.

Negative space may seem a bit abstract to some at first, but as your eyes begin to focus on it you'll quickly realize and appreciate its importance in all design.

Figures 28 and 29 are illustrations of vases you may have seen before as examples of optical illusion. The side edges of the vases define the profiles of two faces. (You may have to stare at these for a while, or squint to focus on

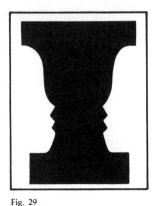

Fig. 28   Fig. 29

Figure 28   Proper margins (negative space) illuminate the positive space.

Figure 29   Crowded margins illuminate the negative space.

the outer edges of the vases.) As you adjust your vision, you will see that the vase (the positive space) is giving shape to the negative space, which in this case we recognize as two faces.

Imagine the vases in Figures 28 and 29 to be or represent the overall silhouette of a block of copy. Notice how the silhouette in Figure 28 is illuminated by the negative space. This is our goal as sign painters — to direct the eye right to the vase without distraction. In Figure 29 there is confusion. The negative space is competing for prominence. Our imagined silhouette of copy is illuminating the negative space by framing it against the edge of the format and causing visual discord.

The vase in Figure 29 is almost harder to see than the profile of the faces. The strong horizontal bars at the top and bottom of the vase seem to graphically relate more to the edges of the format than they do to the silhouette of the vase. This visual phenomenon is an example of compulsive graphic relativity. Figure 29 shows what can go wrong for an artist if he or she isn't aware of negative space and its role of illuminating the positive space.

GRAPHIC PUNCTUATION

Think of using negative space as a form of punctuation. As you do, you will learn to judge proportions of space more successfully. Keep in mind this rule of thumb: If a form has more negative space surrounding it than it has within it, the dominant element will be the positive space. If the proportions of negative space within the form and surrounding it are visually equal, chances are the legibility of your positive form will be diminished. If there is more negative space *within* the form than surrounding it, the negative space within the form, rather than the form itself, will be the dominant element. Due to the many other factors that could modify a particular design, such as color and line value, this rule of thumb does not always apply, but in most cases you will find it very helpful.

Emptiness — negative space — when properly used is rarely seen on a conscious level. In comparing Figures 30 and 31, notice how much easier it is to look at Figure 31. The overall effect is far more natural, as if it was born that way. Figure 30 has a feeling of conflict, and is almost startling to the eye.

Often a feeling of conflict is desirable and appropriate for a specific type of sign, such as a discount promotion, or when you want to create a sense of excitement. However, Figure 30 has too many problems. It has visual impact, but falls short in terms of legibility. The layout conflicts with the format. The lettering and overall silhouette of the composition could have remained the same if there were adequate margins. But due to the fact that it is crowded into the format, pockets of negative space pop out. In particular, note the negative space in the word "Start" between "S" and "t" and between "r" and "t," as well as under the "r"s in "Your Library."

The negative space in Figure 30 is competing graphically with the positive space. To say that the spacing is bad or is too crowded would be a correct observation. However, it would not define the problem in particular, nor would it give you the conceptual awareness to resolve future design problems.

In Figure 31 there is real compatibility between the format and composition. The balance of negative and positive proportional relationships are such that at first glance the eye can enjoy the piece without distraction. You really have to study it with a critical eye before finding hot spots of negative space.

Note the influence of line value (the thickness of the stroke) on the negative space in Figure 31. The negative space within the front loop of the "Y" in "Your" is greater in mass than the space within the "o" or "d" in "Today," and yet is not nearly as strong. It appears as though it is background space or emptiness. On the other hand, the negative space in the "o" and "d" seems isolated or captured by the positive form and no longer feels like background space. It conflicts visually with the letters.

ROLE REVERSAL

The main role of negative space is to flatter the positive form. While this is true, there is also an opposite use for negative space. Keep in mind that the eye can't read everything at once, and that our job is to lead the eye through a composition by highlighting the most important information. One of the tricks in making sure that the secondary copy doesn't compete with the more important copy is to compromise its legibility with negative space.

The double-spaced line "Exceptional Hand Lettered" in Figure 31 is an example of negative space working appropriately as a competing design element. The double spacing creates a monotonous pattern that is stronger than

Fig. 30

Fig. 31

Figure 30 Impact yes, legibility no!

Figure 31 An appealing and remarkable improvement over Figure 30.

any one of the letters or words, interfering with the legibility of the line of copy.

Double-spaced letters like this produce a design effect very similar to the three stars at the bottom of the layout, and can enhance the eye appeal of a sign while making sure that secondary copy doesn't interfere with the more important information.

EYE APPEAL

As you begin to "see" and understand negative space, your eyes will focus on it everywhere. You'll begin to realize that bad layout is very similar to bad letter spacing, which is simply the result of irregular or awkward patterns of positive and negative spaces.

Figure 32 would seem satisfactory to some artists and to most customers — that is, until they're shown an alternative or given a choice of something more visually interesting. This sign checks out okay on the surface. After all, the lettering looks fine — it's centered and there are no mistakes in spelling. So, what's the problem? Figure 32 is visually boring, mechanical, and totally devoid of personality. Even the simplest of signs can and should have eye appeal.

Eye appeal doesn't mean fancy or tricky; it means graphically stimulating. Eye appeal is created by dramatizing the proportional relationships of positive and negative spaces. Note in Figure 32 the monotony of the negative space at the top, middle and bottom of the sign. What's happening in the optical center? Nothing. Do you see how the two words act almost as a frame around the negative space in the center, and frame the negative space against the edges of the format in the left and right side margins?

The first impression of Figure 33 is quite strong. Bang! . . . a cohesive design unit right in the center, forming an immediately recognizable silhouette. Note the harmonious relationship between composition and format as opposed to the discord of Figure 32. See how the negative space in Figure 33 flatters the silhouette and is not working as a competing design element as it is in Figure 32?

Figure 34 has all the same problems that Figure 32 does and is further compromised by the choppy pattern of negative space between the two words.

PRIVATE PARKING

Fig. 32

PRIVATE PARKING

Fig. 33

PRIVATE Parking

Fig. 34

Private PARKING

Fig. 35

Figure 32   Mechanical looking...completely devoid of personality.

Figure 33   A graphic statement that is harmonious with the format.

Figure 34   The irregular pattern of negative space between the two words creates visual discord.

Figure 35   The theoretical straight line at the bottom of the lower case letters in the word "Private" relates harmoniously to the straight line at the top of the capital letters in the word "Parking."

There is truly an unfortunate combination of letter forms in this example.

A line of copy lettered in all capital letters creates the illusion of a straight line at the top and bottom of the words. Lower case letters usually create the illusion of only one straight line, at the bottom of the word. These imaginary straight lines are very influential design elements.

In Figures 32, 33 and 34 notice how the straight line at the top of the word "Private" relates to the top edge of the format. This relationship is more obvious in Figures 32 and 34 due to the negative space in the center of the signs.

Figure 35 is the superior product, because it is visually stimulating. The word "Private" in Figure 35 has only one straight line (at the bottom of the word) and it relates to the optical center and the word "Parking." The uneven rhythm of negative space at the top of the word "Private" is visually independent, not relating at all to the top edge of the format. Use this approach whenever possible in the overall silhouette of a layout, and within a given composition, to ensure the separation of blocks or paragraphs of copy.

5

"Use variation in line value as an illustrator uses foreground, middleground, and background..."

Line Value

Comparing sign design to the illustrative arts is helpful in understanding *line value*. Line value refers to the relative thickness of line in letter strokes, ornamentation, illustration and cartooning. Illustrators and fine artists use color, mass, perspective, a consistent light source and many other elements in their attempt to unify compositions.

As sign designers, we work with a much simpler palette, so to speak. Using line value appropriately can bridge this gap for us. By varying the weight (width) of line we create contrast. When handled properly, contrasting line value can produce many of the same effects that color and perspective produce in illustration.

In lettering, think in terms of three distinct line values: light, medium and

RRR

Figure 36 Contrasting line value can give us many of the same effects that color and perspective produce in illustration.

bold. See Figure 36. (There is a fourth category in typography known as demi-bold. "Demi" means "half.") The following percentages are not exact, but are close enough to carry around in your head and use when you lay out a sign. The stroke of a lightface letter is 10% of its height, medium is 20% and bold is approximately 40%. These percentages do not apply to severely condensed or extended alphabets.

Variation in line value can make a sign more interesting to look at, and is a great aid in leading the eye through the composition. Use variation in line value as illustrators use foreground, middleground and background in their compositions. A light line or stroke is comparable to background, a medium stroke is comparable to middleground, and a bold stroke is comparable to foreground. This comparison helps us determine what weight a line of copy should have, either according to the importance of the information or as a matter of effective design.

One of the most common problems sign painters have in design is monotony of line value and spatial relationships. Unaware of the potential of contrasting line value, and in an attempt to break up a boring composition, they change either the height and color of the letters or change alphabets to the point of distraction. We sometimes do this solely for our own fun and entertainment, whether it's appropriate or not. The mark of a professional is found in the appropriateness of image, and the unity and naturalness of his or her compositions.

CONTRAST

The first chapter of this book explains the necessity of assigning an order of importance to the copy. The idea is to use the most important copy as the graphic focal point, and to let no part graphically compete with another. All copy and design elements have a relative value of importance within a composition, either from an informational or design function point of view.

Contrast is what allows us to distinguish one thing from another. This statement seems so elementary, but few designers demonstrate a conscious awareness of or sensitivity to it. In design, contrast refers to the intensity and dynamics of expression. (This implies a little more than just changing colors or alphabets.) Since we usually work under severe time constraints, we can't spend all day mixing special colors, or making refined sketches. We must

Fig. 37

Fig. 38

Fig. 39

find a way to truly achieve contrast with our limited resources. And there is a way. Since contrast is basically a matter of relative proportions, the shortcut or solution to our problem is in line value — *contrasting* line value!

Figure 37 is an unfortunate composite of mistakes that are commonly made in sign design. You could paint it in any color combination, gold leaf it, sandblast it or illuminate it, and it wouldn't get any better — just more expensive.

Figure 37 is representative of the approach this author used to take: a casual letter on a slant for pizzazz; an upright script because it's fun and fast; a modern alphabet with a creative joining of a few of the letters (a wild and contemporary kind of guy); a little more pizzazz and speed with the angled script overlapping the splashy splash for impact; (one more chance to be cool) the script in the word "Phone"; a couple of straight lines to hold the ad-

Figure 37 A composite of common mistakes in layout.

Figure 38 A well-organized sign that maximizes the use of contrasting line value.

Figure 39 An institutional sign made interesting with the use of contrasting line value.

Embellished Letters
Compliments of Handbook of Early Advertising Art,
Horner/Dover Publishing.

Figure 40   Use light, medium, and bold line values to create a sense of space and depth in your composition.

dress and phone number together; and a striped border around the whole mess.

Figure 38 is a reasonable sketch — not spectacular or terribly creative, but it is appropriate. Notice how the copy is organized and that the sign has three distinct line values. The copy was assigned a line value relative to its importance, and the harmonious relationships were maintained throughout the composition. Figure 38 has symmetry; Figure 37 does not.

Figure 38 illustrates several theories of the use of contrasting line value. One of the most important is the integration of masses. For instance, the reversed panel "Free Classes" looked as if it was pasted on until the light line was striped on the edges. The light line breaks the bold edge of the panel and integrates it with the background. Another positive effect of the light line is that it creates contrast. Before the lines were striped, the lettering and negative space of the panel were too similar in proportion. They produced a very boring and monotonous effect. The thin black line creates contrast and a feeling of decoration.

As I mentioned earlier, it can be very useful to compare what we as sign designers do to what illustrators or fine artists do. Line value is to sign designers what gradation of color is to the illustrator — the passing of one tint or shade of color to another. It is used to create appealing and effective spatial relationships. As sign painters, however, we are required to dramatize things a little more for impact and clarity.

Figure 39 is interesting to the eye, and works simply on the basis of rational layout and contrasting line value. Other than being flush left, it is completely devoid of any tricks or desperate attempts at cleverness. Obviously, this sign wouldn't win any contest — except maybe one, the race to the bank! Even though it's very structured and institutional looking, it is a far superior product to Figure 37, both from the design and production points of view. Figure 39 could be lettered at least as fast, if not faster than Figure 37, and you could probably charge twice as much for it — if for no other reason than as a reward for not ruining IBM's image. Notice how Figure 37 looks as if it was designed by a committee (Mr. Casual, Mr. Script and Mr. Hack), as compared to the continuity of Figures 38 and 39.

The pregnant woman in Figure 40 is an example of contrasting line value in illustration. The drawing is just good enough to create a sense of space, which is the key to its believability. The drawing would have greater appeal if there was a more definite middleground. Compare this illustration to the word "Received." Notice how the word "Received" and its ornamentation provide a greater sense of space or depth of field than the illustration of the woman. It has a definite foreground, middleground and background.

The "Z" in Figure 40 is the closest equivalent to the daily work of a sign painter. It doesn't have the obvious sense of space that the other examples have. It takes a little closer study. To my eye, it appears as though the middleground is too bold, and thus competes with the foreground.

By creating a sense of space and depth in your composition you transport viewers into the sign. They are no longer just looking at a flat surface with symbols painted on it; they are now involved subliminally with space and realism, which heightens their interest. The value of creating a sense of space in your composition is comparable to the "Chrome Look" in lettering, which has been popular for the last several years. The reason it is so appealing is its believability. It has form and depth, which attracts and holds our attention as no flat-appearing surface could.

The eye is stimulated by contrasting line value and a sense of depth. Contrasting line value has universal appeal. A good example of this phenomenon is the popularity of calligraphy . . . script, roman letters or so-called "Old English." How many people want their names lettered in a gothic style? People enjoy well-balanced thick and thin letters, and compositions with contrasting line value.

THREAD OF THE FABRIC

Use Figure 41 to appreciate and understand line value from a different perspective. Starting at the top of the format, scan through the composition to the bottom of the sign. Imagine your eyes to be the wind and the lines of lettering to be wind barriers. Notice how the lighter strokes allow your eyes to "blow" through to the heavier strokes. Repeat the same exercise from the bottom up.

The wind barriers represent visual stops, relative to the importance of the copy. The eye cannot read everything at once. It must be permitted to flow through and scan the sign. Figure 41 also demonstrates how contrasting line

Figure 41 Note how contrasting line value was used to prioritize the copy.

value creates rhythm and modifies masses (copy blocks). Note how the layout begins and ends with a lightface letter. This serves to soften the silhouette of the copy, preventing it from competing with the edge of the stylized format.

A black and white sketch such as Figure 41 is ideal in helping us to understand the role of line value in design. The black background absorbs light, while the white lettering reflects it. Gradations of value and color are produced by the intensity of the reflection of light. If we wanted to add color to this sign, and maintain the same priority of thought, we would probably have to modify the line value to compensate for the reflective qualities of a particular color. Cool colors tend to recede, while warm colors, because they reflect more light, advance or expand in effect. In planning your line value, keep in mind the effect of color and the illusion of size it produces.

A sensitivity to line value and the ability to manipulate it will give you a new control over layout and design. It will give you the freedom and dexterity of a full spectrum palette. You'll be able to play light against dark for drama and clarity without changing colors or alphabets. Your layouts will look more natural and interesting as you begin to think in terms of integrating masses by implying gradation with contrasting line value. Perhaps most importantly, we will all begin to think and work from an aesthetic point of view instead of the "tricks of the trade" mentality that has kept the sign business in the dark ages.

The mark of professional layout is clarity and cleanliness. No matter how involved or ornate the individual elements may be, they can be assigned a priority and integrated into a singular whole. Line value is the thread of the fabric.

"...harmonious rhythms unify a composition."

Rhythm

The term *rhythm* has several definitions, all of which can help to shed some light on this phenomenon. In graphics, the simplest definition is: "A pattern, sense of direction or illusion of movement created by lines, forms and colors." Rhythm can result from any one of these elements individually, and from their combination. In learning to see and understand rhythm as a design element, you will note that most compositions have two rhythms: dominant and subordinate. Rhythms are either harmonious or conflicting. The same is true of individual letters and groups of letters.

Since this book is printed in black and white, rhythm cannot be illustrated here in terms of color. Most of what we have discussed about line and form is also true of color, and you will find it easy to make the comparisons.

To appreciate rhythm as a design element requires a lot more insight and information than a simple definition of the term. The artist must be advanced enough in his or her perception to see more than just the positive space. An appreciation of negative space and an understanding of the phenomenon of compulsive graphic relativity are essential. Rhythm is a *relative* phenomenon. Its essence is contextual; what has meaning or rightness in one instance may have no meaning or be inappropriate in another. (This is a theoretical point for the record; don't let it slow you down for now. It will be more easily understood with the help of the figures on the following pages.)

A general definition of rhythm could be: "The relationship and interdependence of parts with reference to one another, and to the artistic whole." Once you see it as a design element, rhythm will have the same impact on your perception as negative space.

RHYTHM IN FORMAT AND LAYOUT

The first thing you see when you look at Figure 42 is conflicting rhythms. Which conflicting rhythms? There are two elements of almost equal value creating visual discord. Before reading any further, analyze Figure 42 and determine for yourself what the problem is. Take a piece of white paper and cover all of the copy on the sign, except "Deluxe, 200 to 700 sq. ft." Gradually lower the paper, revealing one line of copy at a time. As you go along notice where things start to fall apart.

The first real problem is the visual conflict between the "e" in the word "Space" and the black panel at the bottom of the sign. Compare the phrase "Office Space" in Figures 42 and 43 and notice how "Office Space" in Figure 43 reads graphically as an independent unit. The silhouette of these words creates a horizontal rhythm that is allowed to express itself without interruption. In Figure 42, that very same rhythm is in conflict with the reversed panel at the bottom of the sign. The conflict between this silhouette and the reversed panel is further complicated by the phenomenon of compulsive graphic relativity. (Do you see it?) The "e" in "Space" relates almost as much to the reversed panel as it does to its own thought group. This conflicting area in Figure 42 ("Office Space" and the panel) suffers from a double dose of inconsistent compulsive graphic relativity — the rhythm of the silhouette and the letter "e" are both conflicting design elements.

Fig. 42   Fig. 43   Fig. 44

The secret to good layout is organization and clarity. Rhythms serve to unite a composition and make it more interesting to the eye. Harmonious rhythms lead the eye through a layout, while conflicting rhythms tend to stop it and call attention to a particular element within the whole. This discussion concerns only cause and effect, rather than denoting good or bad; there are times when visual conflict is desirable.

As I mentioned in the first chapter, there are two fundamental choices in layout. The first is to lay out and letter something that looks natural and visually pleasing within a given format. The second approach is to do something so visually strong and overpowering that it causes the format to recede (a Super Graphic). In natural layout, the dominant rhythm is determined by the direction of the format, generally vertical or horizontal. The silhouette of the overall copy area must be consistent with the rhythm of the format. Super Graphics produce a dominant rhythm independent of the format.

Figure 42 An example of conflicting rhythms.

Figure 43 A remarkably clean composition, although the reversed panel at the bottom of the sign is a little too close to the center of the sign. If it were 20% smaller, the contrast between the white panel and the black panel would be more interesting to the eye.

Figure 44 Note that each line of copy has a horizontal rhythm. To integrate this pattern with the vertical format, the lines of copy were tightly spaced to form a vertical silhouette that is harmonious with the shape of the format.

Of the three sketches above, Figure 44 best illustrates a harmonious rhythm between the copy silhouette and the format. It also demonstrates what may appear to some to be a contradiction — that is, all the lines of copy have a horizontal rhythm in a vertical format. This contradiction of rhythms works because the rhythm of the overall silhouette is just strong enough to reinforce and flatter the format, rendering the rhythm of the lettering subordinate. The eye appeal of this example in fact results from the conflict that is created by the contrasting vertical and horizontal rhythms. (However, this sketch would be better if the letter spacing was tighter and the line value was bolder in "Deluxe Office Space.")

Both Figures 42 and 43 suffer from the same problem. The reversed subordinate panels at the bottom of each sign compromise the rhythm of the format. They are too big. The rhythm of the top edge of these subordinate formats are so close to the center of the sign that they tend to cut the signs in half. Both signs would be more effective if the vertical rhythm of the format was allowed to express itself.

Recurring rhythms are used to lead the eye through the layout. They may be of positive space or negative space, or both. Perhaps the easiest to see, and to learn to use, are recurring rhythms of line value — light, medium and bold.

Figure 43 demonstrates the power of recurring rhythms of line value. Even though the format has been almost cut in half, creating two separate signs, the magic of recurring rhythms is just strong enough to hold the entire composition together. Notice how the medium line value of "Deluxe" relates to the phone number, the light line of the square footage relates to the word "Properties," and the bold stroke of "Office Space" relates to "Merit."

Check out the recurring line value in Figure 44. Is it too busy? Would it have been better to make "Deluxe Office Space" all the same weight?

RHYTHM IN LETTERING

Letter styles (typefaces or fonts, if you prefer) fall into two basic categories or functions — text (body copy) and display (headings). Text alphabets are designed primarily for legibility, with image or mood being of secondary consideration. They are usually neutral and may be used in most circumstances. Display alphabets offer a great deal of latitude and room for creative expression. They are designed specifically to suggest an image or mood. The ability to distinguish between the two and use them appropriately separates the professional from the amateur.

Dominant, harmonious rhythms unify a composition, beginning with the smallest unit — a letter. Consistency in rhythm determines the success or failure of a layout. All lettering, to a lesser or greater degree, contains both harmonious and conflicting rhythms. Text alphabets are consistently harmonious, while the dominant rhythm of display alphabets may be harmonious *or* conflicting, even to the extreme.

The market is flooded with display alphabets, and most of them are poorly designed. This statement is not meant to take a shot at type designers, but rather to point out the power of rhythm in design. The success and acceptance of display alphabets is not based upon the quality of design in the individual characters so much as the image and rhythms they create. Their best use is in very short headings with lots of air space around them. The eye appeal of display alphabets is a matter of dramatic proportion and rhythm. We all have experienced seeing something very powerful and appealing to the eye at first glance, only to notice, upon closer inspection, the inferior quality of the individual parts.

Figure 45-A has to be one of the worst alphabets ever conceived. This figure is very confusing; it is not clear whether the dominant rhythm is in the silhouette of the word or in the bold vertical strokes. In fact, when you squint and look at it, the negative space in the "e" and "c" becomes so strong it almost separates "Special" into two words. This is an extreme example of inferior rhythms.

Figure 45-B illustrates a common problem in casual lettering. Note the inconsistent rhythms in the first example. Each letter looks like an independent design, with little reference to the next. The second example demonstrates superior rhythms, both horizontally and vertically.

The two examples in Figure 45-C are more subtle in their differences. The first example, an accurate rendition of Cooper Black, looks weak, due to what this author considers to be original design flaws. Compare all the letters in this example and notice the differences in the serifs. In the second example, notice that each letter appears stronger and that the ambiguous and conflicting rhythms have been minimized.

SPECIAL

Fig. 45-A

SPECIAL

SPECIAL

Fig. 45-B

Special

Special

Fig. 45-C

SPECIAL

SPECIAL

Fig. 45-D

Special

Special

Fig. 45-E

Figure 45 Notice the subtle differences in letter forms that enhance rhythms within words.

In Figure 45-D notice how the rhythm of the straight line at the top and bottom of the letters has been enhanced in the second, gothic version by the way the "s," "e," "c" and "a" have been handled.

Figure 45-E is left for you to analyze. In summary, rhythm is a pattern, a sense of direction, or illusion of movement created by lines, forms and colors. The dominant rhythms of your composition should be consistent with the order of thought and serve to unify your layout.

"...it is better to change alphabets than to distort one of the originals."

7

Selecting Alphabets

This chapter will focus on the design function of and the differences between upper and lower case letters. Traditional wisdom has held that it's best to limit yourself to two alphabets, with possibly a third for a company logo. This is good advice with which I have always agreed and generally practice. However, the rule can and must be broken occasionally. If you understand why the rule exists artistically, you may break it at will. Every sign is unique. You must have the freedom to do whatever is necessary to achieve an integrated whole. In art, it's the results that count.

"BUSY" MEANS CONFLICTING

Most rules and principles in design may be broken, once you fully understand their intention. The advice to limit a sign to two alphabets was necessary in the old days for several reasons. Perhaps the two most important were the incompatibility of the known letter styles with each other, and the design or layout skills of the average sign painter. Their signs frequently looked "busy," not just with the addition of a second or third alphabet, but with the addition of the second or third word. This problem gave rise to the second commandment of sign painting — "Limit your composition to two alphabets." (The first is to spell it right.)

Our growth as sign designers has been severely limited by our down-home terminology. The word "busy" is used universally in the sign business to describe a composition that is confusing, or that has too much going on in it. If the term "busy" means a sign is bad, then does that mean you can fix it by making it "idle"? Wouldn't it be more accurate to say a composition is "conflicting" instead of busy? Without correctly identifying the problem, we will never find the solution. When you realize that the rule of using just two alphabets per sign is based on possible visual and design conflict, you say, "Okay, I'll use as few alphabets as possible, but as many as may be necessary, without creating conflict."

ELIMINATE EQUALITY

We select alphabets on the basis of image appropriateness and the amount of space available. Whatever the words, we have to make them fit and look good within a particular format. In order to create pleasing silhouettes with our copy blocks, it is sometimes necessary to use potentially conflicting alphabets.

Conflict in design occurs when two or more elements are simultaneously competing for your attention. In order to compete, their size must be fairly equal and their shapes rhythmically incompatible. One solution to the problem of conflict, then, is to *eliminate equality*. You can do this by reducing either the size, line value or contrast of color (tonal value) of the competing elements.

In recognition of the need to create pleasing silhouettes of copy, the rule of using just two alphabets per sign is cautiously dumped. Medium or heavy copy signs frequently require three or four nonconflicting alphabets to create a pleasing composition. More often than not, it is better to change alphabets than to distort one of the originals. The distortion of a previously used alphabet tends to look more like poor letter construction or bad spacing than like planned design.

A line of upper and lower case letters is easier to read than a line of all capital letters. The all-capital version forms a visual barrier which interferes with the recognition of the individual letters. Capital letters form a theoretical straight line at the top and bottom of a word, sentence or thought group. Consequently, the eye must first dismiss this design element before it can read individual letters and words. See Figure 47.

Notice in the upper and lower case example that there is only one hard line, at the bottom. The top of the lettering is open without the imaginary straight line. There is ample negative space, making each individual letter much more legible.

The second reason why a combination of upper and lower case letters is more legible is that the rhythm of positive and negative spaces is more pleasing and harmonious than in an all-capital line of letters.

Compare the two examples in Figure 48. In the all-capital version, notice the variety of shapes and sizes of the positive and negative spaces. These different shapes and sizes compete with each other, creating design conflict and visual discord. On the other hand, the lower case example is more consistent in these shapes and sizes, making it more harmonious and easier to read.

Upper and lower case letters are not only more legible than all-capital letters, but are also more interesting to the eye. The shapes of lower case letters are informal and closer to the shapes found in nature. They are friendlier in appearance and easier to live with than the regimented look of all capitals.

The imaginary straight line at the top and bottom of capital letters and at the bottom of lower case letters is a very important design element. It defines the silhouette of the word or thought group and almost acts as a magnet. That is, it visually relates to, or draws to itself, any other real or imaginary line that is not separated from it by ample air space.

This imaginary line is a key factor in deciding whether to use all capitals or upper and lower case letters. Notice in Figure 49 how the two adjoining imaginary lines of the capital letters relate to each other. In Figure 50 there is conflict between the bottom line of the capital letters and the ascenders of the

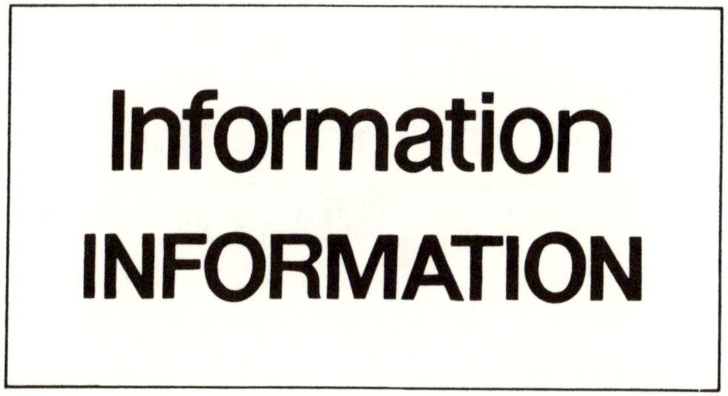

Fig. 46

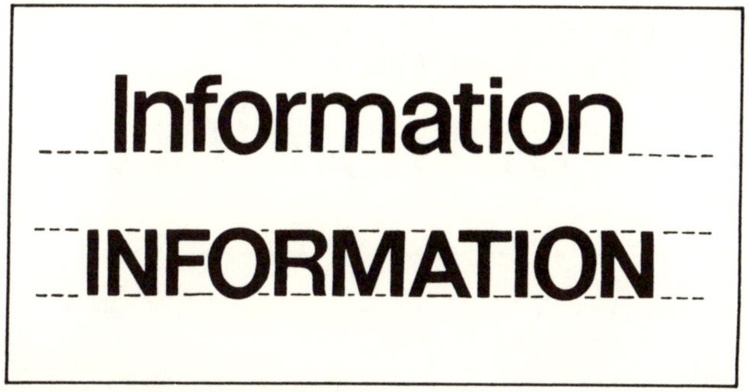

Fig. 47

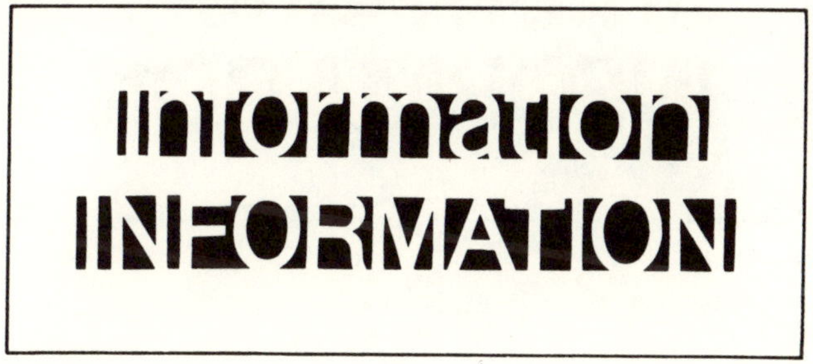

Fig. 48

Figure 46 A combination of upper and lower case letters is easier to read than a line of capital letters.

Figure 47 Capital letters form a theoretical straight line at the top and bottom of a word. The upper and lower case example has only one theoretical straight line, at the bottom.

Figure 48 Rhythms of positive and negative space are more harmonious in lower case lettering.

INFORMATION
INFORMATION

Fig. 49

INFORMATION
Information

Fig. 50

Information
INFORMATION

Fig. 51

Figure 49   The imaginary straight lines in capital letters relate to each other.

Figure 50   There is visual conflict between the bottom line of the capital letters and the ascenders of the lower case letters.

Figure 51   The imaginary straight line at the bottom of the lower case letters relates well to the straight line at the top of the capital letters.

lower case letters. The only reason the words relate to each other is that there is more negative space in the margins than there is between them, forcing them to form a single silhouette. Figure 51 demonstrates the correct relationship when using a combination of all capital and upper and lower case letters. The imaginary line at the bottom of the lower case letters in Figure 51 relates well to the imaginary line at the top of the capital letters.

I use these imaginary lines to make sure thought groups and copy blocks hang together. I use the uneven and open space above lower case letters to make sure things don't relate. For example, in Figure 51 the lower case word "Information" does not relate at all to the top edge of the format. Instead, it relates to the optical center, due to the imaginary straight line at the bottom of the word. Finally, any sign design should be architecturally sound. Compare Figures 50 and 51 — you'll see that Figure 50 is top-heavy.

As mentioned before, a simplified way of defining layout is to just consider it to be the process of assembling copy blocks or thought groups. To the extent you are able to give definite shape to these blocks, the easier it will be to create visually pleasing compositions. Sign painters have long recognized the value of using design panels to control their layouts. It is easier to divide a sign into three panel areas and come up with a unified composition than it is to lay out raw copy in a pleasing manner. Design panels can be very effective, and a great lifesaver. However, on a scale of one to ten in difficulty or design accomplishment, the ability to arrange design panels rates a three. (The layout within the panels rates a ten!)

The true ability of an artist shows up in the most routine work. Concentrate on organizing your copy. Form definite, pleasing silhouettes with your copy blocks. Arrange them within the format so that they look architecturally sound. Avoid using design panels for a while; they can quickly become a crutch.

THE "RIGHT PLACE"

Another way to think about the use of lower case lettering is similar to the discussion in chapter 5 on the use and interpretation of line value. Reread the suggested exercise and observations of Figure 41 (Thread of the Fabric). The imaginary straight line at the top of capital letters may be viewed as a visual stop or barrier. The lower case letters are open at the top, and allow the eye

Fig. 52

Fig. 53

Fig. 54

to go through to the next line without hesitation.

Figure 52 is a sketch of a showcard for a hotel lobby. Note the way the copy is organized and the use of upper and lower case lettering. "Pinata Restaurant/Breakfast Buffet" forms a single copy block. The lettering style of "Pinata" and the two doodads on each side comprise their logo. The lightface Microgramma lettering for the word "Restaurant" and the Cooper style lettering for "Breakfast Buffet" were my choices. Three different alphabets right in the optical center of the sign. Why don't they conflict with each other? Because they are so radically different in size, each word looks like it belongs just where it sits. This showcard contains five different type styles. Does it look "busy"?

Figure 53 has seven different type styles. There is a certain amount of visual conflict in this sign, but I wouldn't say it looks "busy." The design conflict between "Easter Sunday" and "Brunch" is visually stimulating. Actually, the

Figure 52 Visual conflict between alphabets can be minimized by controlling the line value. Play light against bold or medium line values.

Figure 53 Conflicting rhythms can be visually stimulating.

Figure 54 Extreme visual conflict is undesirable in signage.

apparent conflict is in the nature of the condensed lettering in the word "Brunch." Tightly spaced capital letters like this form a strong horizontal shape that conflicts with the vertical thrust of each individual letter. There is just enough harmony between the horizontal rhythm of the lettering in "Easter Sunday," and the horizontal rhythm of the silhouette of the word "Brunch," to make this combination of letter styles work.

CONTRAST — NOT CONFLICT

Theoretically, the script in the word "Fabulous" in Figure 53 could have been a poor choice of alphabet. If it were any larger or bolder in size, it would conflict with the lettering in the word "Easter." In selecting alphabets, it is important to keep in mind that you are looking for contrasting styles, not alphabets that are similar in nature. For example, the informality of the shapes and thick and thin strokes of the lettering in "Fabulous" and "Easter" are not contrasting, they are competitive. Contrasting alphabets include formal against informal, thick and thin letters against gothic, serif against sans serif styles, a regular face against an extended or condensed typeface.

Figure 54 has nine different alphabets . . . and it almost worked. It is conflicting and hard to read, not because there are too many alphabets, but because of the poor choice of letter style in the word "Bio," and the distracting use of the dashes.

The rule of thumb that guides us in the number of alphabets that may be used in a sign is *design function*. How is that particular alphabet going to look in that particular space? If it is proportionately and rhythmically consistent with the space available, without conflicting with any other alphabet in use, then it is probably okay. Notice the bottom block of copy in Figure 53. It has three alphabets that, with the aid of the decorative lines, form a nice solid silhouette. The three alphabets work together because each is in a "place" that is proportionately appropriate for its form and style.

Alphabets

The following alphabets are practical for sign painting and showcard writing. They are versatile and adaptable to most routine signage. Commit them to memory and develop the ability to extend or condense them as needed.

ABCDEFGHIJKLM
NOPQRSTUVWXYZ
1234567890&!?
abcdefhijklmnop
qrstug,vwxyz

This sans serif roman alphabet was inspired by the typeface "Optima." It has been modified to enhance rhythms of positive and negative spaces. It is relatively quick to execute, and appropriate for many different projects. On a good day, it can be rendered as a single stroke letter. Upper and lower case letters, tightly spaced, can look very elegant — or you can get loose with them and become very informal and playful. See next page for examples.

Dawn Marie

gift 2nd 53066

NOW

BOLD MEDIUM LIGHT

...real... work 9

HORSE

An ideal alphabet for most design projects

BEAUTIFUL

Sans Serif

ROMAN

This alphabet is Versatile

ORIGINAL 13½ × 18"

REMEMBER THE GOLDEN RULE

modification OF CHARACTERS

FOR FUN!

DOUBLE SPACE FOR EFFECT!

ABCDEFG
HIKLMNOP
QRSTUV
WXYZ

abcdefghijklmnopqrrstuvwxyz

abcdefghijklmnopqrrstuvwxyz

Script is a fun alphabet, loaded with opportunity for self-expression. The script illustrated here can be rendered to look formal or informal, with slight modifications. The strokes remain basically the same for either effect; it's just a matter of regimenting the rhythms for a formal look, and loosening up for an informal style. This script was lettered with a chisel-edged brush, single stroke. See next page for examples and basic strokes.

Special Task

Reservations Oan!

Christmas Beautiful!

bold O

Dawn Marie

The surest way to corrupt a young man... is to teach him to esteem more highly those who think alike than those who think differently.

Happy Birthday!

N·I·E·T·Z·S·C·H·E

THE Basic Strokes

ABCcm

abcdEfghijklm

Original

11¼"x15"

ABCDEFGHIJKL
MNOPQRSTUVWXYZ
abcdefghijklmnopqrstuvwyz;
$1234567890!?&

This is an old standby alphabet that has several updated versions. This older style is presented for a couple of reasons. First, it represents the basic form that the others are derived from, and secondly, it's faster and has greater utility. We used to refer to this single stroke letter as "Gas Pipe" or "Stove Pipe." If you can handle this alphabet and maintain its rhythm and proportions, you'll be better equipped to render the more contemporary versions, correcting their many awkward and inconsistent relationships.

Vary height! NOT ONLY THE and WIDTH OF ALL LETTER BUT ALSO THE LINE VALUE FOR CONTRAST

ABCDEFGHIJK
LMNOPQRSTU
VWXYZ,?!&
abcdefghijklmnopqrstuvwxyz
1234567890

This is one of the easiest roman alphabets to letter. The obvious patterns of thick and thin strokes are clear to see and understand. Its uniformity facilitates good spacing and consistent rhythms of positive and negative spaces. This alphabet offers plenty of opportunity for improvisation. You may expand or condense it, create formal and informal effects, use swash capital letters, etc. Play with it and have fun!

Beauty is the reflection of...

SYMMETRY

THE EXCELLENCE OF POSITIVE & NEGATIVE PROPORTIONAL

RELATIONSHIPS

A B G K { ORIGINAL 11½"x15"

ABCDEFGHIJ
KLMNOPQRS
TUVWXYZ!?
abcdefghijklmno
pqrstuvwxyz

Casual lettering is a fun, fast and very personal alphabet which works well in light, medium and bold line values. Care should be taken, however, not to overuse it. Think of Casual as a display alphabet, rather than a text alphabet. When used in the "discount" type of showcard, it can get pretty loose. Some letters may touch and even overlap occasionally. Casual lettering is most effective when used in conjunction with a gothic letter for contrast. Think in terms of using dramatic, "snappy" lettering with Casual, not cartooning.

WARNING :

INAPPROPRIATE OR *Excessive* USE OF
CASUAL LETTERING, MAY CAUSE **WARTS**

ABCDEFGHIJKLMN
OPQRSTUVWXYZ!?
,,
abcdefghijklmnopqrs
tuvwxyz, & 12345678

ABCDEFGHIJ
KLMNOPQRST
UVWXYZ
abcdefghijklmno
pqrstuvwxyz

This alphabet is very similar to Cooper Black, but has been modified to enhance rhythms of positive and negative spaces. It should be considered a display alphabet, and generally used only for headlines. It's versatile and lends itself to artistic license. You can use swashes in the capital letters or exaggerate certain other characteristics. See next page for possibilities. In most circumstances, a combination of upper and lower case letters looks best as opposed to all caps.

Fr★ntier Sale

CELEBRATION

extended!

BOLD

Sunday Brunch

ORIGINAL . . . 9 X 12½"

ABCDEFGHI
JKLMNOPQ
RSTUVWXYZ

abcdefghijk
lmnopqrstuv
wxyz !?,

This display alphabet has a lot of personality. Basically, it is a
single stroke letter, rendered with the tip of an oversized and very
wet brush. A three-fingered grip makes this alphabet relatively easy
to execute. It looks equally good in a light or medium face, and as
with most casual lettering, it looks good when played against a
more disciplined alphabet.

Today's Menu

Special lettering

announce Music

Pacific Atlantic

"Fats Domino"

ABCDEFGHIJKLMN OPQRSTUVWXYZ

abcdefghijklmnop qrstuvwxyz

This alphabet was originally inspired by Caslon Italic, but in my own work has gradually evolved in appearance towards Century Italic. It may be used as a display or a text alphabet. The thin strokes are made with the contracted tip of the brush. With a little luck and some touch-up, the bold stroke can be rendered in a single stroke (up to about a 3½" letter).

1234567890?!$

"...and as you dream, so shall you become. Your Vision is the promise of what you shall one day be..." JAMES ALLEN / AS A MAN THINKETH

Thank You Lynn!

ABCDEFG
HIJKLMNOP
QRSTUVW
XYZ?!&

abcdefghijklmn
opqrstuvwxyz

This is one of my favorite alphabets. It has a lot of impact and works well for short headings. It may be extended or condensed to fit almost any format. For a super bold letter it has excellent rhythms of positive and negative spaces. I prefer to use a combination of upper and lower case letters with this alphabet. A heading lettered in all caps may form too hard of an imaginary line at the top and bottom of a line of copy, thus diminishing its legibility.

ABCDEFG HIJKLMNOP QRSTUVW XYZ & ?

abcdefghijklmn opqrstuvwxyz

This extended alphabet is a take-off on Microgramma. It is a display alphabet, but may be used occasionally for text. This, or a similar extended style, should be a part of every sign painter's repertoire. It looks good in light, medium, or bold line values.

ABCDEFGHIJ
KLMNOPQRS
TUVWXYZ

abcdefghi jklmno
pqrstuvwxyz

This display alphabet is a modified Cooper Black Italic. It looks best when used in a combination of upper and lower case letters. It can be rendered to look formal or informal. The lettering on this page was allowed to expand, and to loosen up a bit to show its informal potential. Compare the rhythms of this version with those of the original Cooper Black Italic.

ABCDEFGHIJKLM
NOPQRSTUVWXYZ
1234567890 !?&;
★★
abcdefghijklmno
pqrstuvwxyz

This theatrical showcard alphabet may be used for headings or text. The idea is to get loose with it. It can be very expressive and modified to fit your needs. It's essentially a single stroke letter that's squared off at the top and bottom of each stroke. Long words or sentences should be in upper and lower case letters for legibility.

ABCDEFGHIJK
LMNOPQRSTUVWXYZ
1234567890 !?&

aabcdeefgghijklm
nopqrstuvwxyz

This light face, text alphabet is very fast. It's ideal for showcard work or general sign painting. It may be lettered with an even stroke (gothic), or as a roman letter, with slight thick and thin characteristics. Use the tip of an oversized, wet brush for speed. Tight letter spacing, or double spacing looks best with this alphabet.

8

"To understand and use color effectively, a sign painter must first master the fine points of layout."

Color

On the whole, we make better choices in color than we do in layout. In layout, it has been "Do your own thing! One person's opinion is as good as another's." The reason we have self-control in the use of color, and not in layout, is that we all know there are principles and complex theories of color. They intimidate us, and keep us at the conservative end of the spectrum.

The science of color *is* complex, but the good news is that we don't need a complete theoretical understanding of color to be good sign painters. Common sense, the knowledge of a few elementary laws of color, and a sensitivity to cultural expectations will distinguish our work.

The interesting thing is that, although few of us realize it, color is something we've grown up with and worked with all our lives. There is no need to go into the emotional and psychological connotations of color. Nearly everyone knows that red can imply anger and blue is a good color for ice.

Your choice of color should be based on image appropriateness and effectiveness. Red and black on white are a traditional "bread and butter" color combination that will always have its place in signage. Some sign people advocate avoiding these colors because they are boring or unimaginative. However, so-called "boring" colors are more a problem of monotony of relative proportions (line value and layout) than of color.

To understand and use color effectively, a sign painter must first master the fine points of layout. Without skill in layout, an artist cannot view the use of color in a reasonable context. How can one appreciate red and black on white when they are used with inferior letter forms and bad layout?

All colors have relative value on a scale of light and dark. The relative value of a color is where most sign painters have trouble. We tend to confuse the brightness or intensity of a color with the more fundamental issue of contrasting values. An example would be the comparison of bright red and fire red against a white background in bulletin colors. Bright red is the darker value, and thus strikes a greater contrast with white than does the lighter fire red. Up close, fire red commands attention and has more pizzazz, but from a distance, bright red will be more legible.

It's important to keep in mind that color is but one element of design. Color alone does not make a good sign, but color alone can destroy an otherwise good design. Color must always be thought of as a part of the "whole." The typical mistake is to plan a composition around color alone. Color is the servant and representative of ideas, not the idea itself. Naturally we have a color scheme in mind before we start designing or laying out a sign. However, if you truly want to maximize the effectiveness of your color, lay out the sign completely and correctly before painting it.

Edit and determine the relative importance of the copy. Form thought groups and select alphabets. Arrange and develop pleasing silhouettes of copy, keeping in mind the idea of foreground, middleground and background through the use of line value and tonal values. Now that your composition is established . . . bring it to life with color!

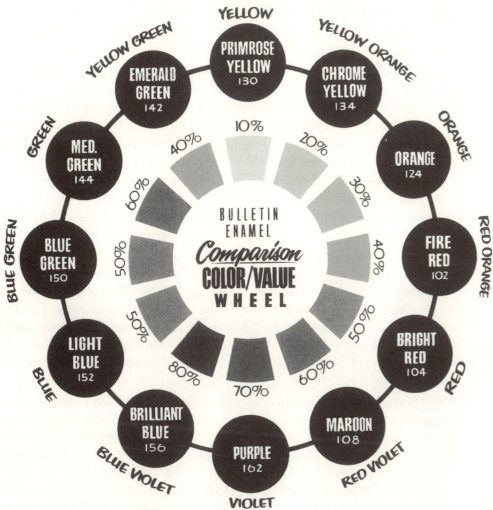

YELLOW

YELLOW GREEN

YELLOW ORANGE

GREEN

ORANGE

BLUE GREEN

RED ORANGE

BLUE

RED

BLUE VIOLET

RED VIOLET

VIOLET

EMERALD GREEN 142

PRIMROSE YELLOW 130

CHROME YELLOW 134

MED. GREEN 144

ORANGE 124

BLUE GREEN 150

FIRE RED 102

LIGHT BLUE 152

BRIGHT RED 104

BRILLIANT BLUE 156

PURPLE 162

MAROON 108

BULLETIN ENAMEL *Comparison* COLOR/VALUE WHEEL

10% 20% 30% 40% 50% 60% 70% 80% 40% 50% 60% 70%

Figure 55

THE COLOR WHEEL

Figure 55 is a color wheel showing the actual names of the primary, second-ary and intermediate colors (lettered around the outside edge) and the names of their corresponding bulletin colors (lettered in the black circles). As sign painters, we might as well be realistic about our color wheel and think in terms of the potentials of bulletin enamels. Due to the chemistry involved, many of the more vibrant colors used in printing and the graphic arts simply aren't possible for us to mix and match.

The inner circle in Figure 55 is a value wheel I composed that corresponds to the bulletin enamels. Value is the relative darkness or lightness of a color. For example, according to this wheel, orange is 30% of the value of black. An important note: These observations of relative value are not scientific; they are merely estimates.

If you are serious about color, I suggest you make up your own color and value wheel using bulletin colors. Most sign painters just use a color chart for inspiration. Now that I've been forced to make one up for instructional and theoretical purposes, I see its real benefit. The color wheel educates you to the theoretical possibilities, while the color chart caters to our whims. It is best to use both.

To work with the color wheel, it is necessary to know its terms and definitions. *Hue* is a pure color. From now on I'll use the terms hue and color interchangeably. When I mention a particular color, it will be a bulletin color — our enamel substitute for the legitimate hue.

The colors on our wheel are separated into three categories. *Primary colors* are primrose yellow, bright red and light blue. *Secondary colors* are medium green, orange and purple. The remaining colors are called *intermediates*.

A *tint* is produced when white is added to an original hue. Many of the bulletin colors tend to gray a little when you add white to them. To eliminate some of this problem, try also adding a little of the closest warm color on the wheel. This is especially effective if your intention was to create a highlight of color. The only exception to this would occur when you wish to make a tint of blue-green. Since medium green is too dark in value, skip it and add emerald green to lighten the blue-green. Colors that are light in value make the best tints.

Theoretically, a *shade* is produced when black is added to a hue, but caution must be used when adding black to a bulletin color. Generally it works only with the cooler hues. The warmer colors tend to change color rather than get darker. To create a shade of a warm color, try adding a cooler version of the color with just a touch of black. Do not mix black with any of the yellows, unless you want an earthy green. Colors that are dark in value make the best shades. Black and a little red will turn most colors into an earth tone.

To *tone* a color is to add gray to it, which can be an effective technique. For instance, to create a feeling of real pizzazz in the main copy of a sign, letter it in a pure hue against a toned background or color scheme.

Complementary colors are the exact opposites on the color wheel. *Split complements* are the two hues that lie next to the exact opposite of a color. For example, light blue is the complementary color of orange on our wheel, and blue-green and brilliant blue are its split complements.

Complementary colors play warm against cool. Split complements offer greater choice and are more attractive than complementary colors. Note that warm and bright colors look best in small areas set against large areas of cool colors. In signage, warm colors should be planned to appear in front of cool colors. Warm colors appear to expand or come forward, while cool colors appear to recede. This same phenomenon is observable in the different line values, and in a light-to-dark value scale. See Figure 56.

Adjacent colors (colors next to each other on the wheel) always tend to look good together. However, if they are close in value, such as light blue and blue-green, one of the colors should be modified to enhance their contrast. *Analogous* colors are any set of three, and sometimes four, adjacent colors on our wheel.

A *monochromatic* color scheme is rendered with one hue, utilizing tints, shades and tones. Monochromatic color schemes can be very elegant, or in the case of earth tones, create an aged and weathered look.

The color wheel has four *triads* of harmonious color combinations: 1. the primary colors — bright red, primrose yellow and light blue; 2. the secondary colors — orange, medium green and purple; 3. the intermediates fire red, emerald green and brilliant blue, and 4. the intermediates chrome yellow, blue-green and maroon. You can get into a lot of trouble with these intense color combinations, especially with the triad of secondary colors. The successful use of triads is a delicate matter of proportional relationships.

A color wheel in black and white, or the terms and the theoretical association of colors is hardly inspirational . . . or is it? What if the information in the few preceding paragraphs was almost all the theoretical base a sign painter would need to "think" his way through his career? Would that not give one a sense of hope, power and control?

The simple act of planning and making your own color wheel will educate you. Try it! Talk your way through the aforementioned principles of color a couple of times, and you'll never be intimidated by the subject again. You may not have all the answers on the tip of your tongue, but through the use of the color wheel and a Pantone color mixing guide you'll know how to find them.

COLOR PHILOSOPHY

The study and the intelligent use of color is a philosophy. You cannot become a top-notch designer without a conscious philosophy of function, form and color. You must have a goal and a standard, not to limit your view, but to expand it. Color is one of the easier studies for sign painters because it's not abstract. You don't have to learn to see color, but you do have to develop a rational philosophy of its use. Color is much easier to understand and control than the abstract elements of layout.

This philosophy is called common sense. It has to do with the way we see or think about things, which is — one thing at a time! The brain will acknowledge many perceptions simultaneously, but not coherently. The designer's role is to unify and prioritize visual information consistent with the brain's ability to understand it. The function of color is to attract the eye and reinforce a message on an emotional level without overloading the brain.

How do you use color so that it will not alarm or overload the brain? By using it as it is experienced in reality — foreground, middleground and background. However, we don't consciously experience foreground, middleground and background. Rather, we experience a *unified* whole, a panorama. All things visually meld together, and are naturally prioritized in nature. There is a natural perspective and integration of colors outdoors. Despite the multitude of colors, there is order and harmony! In effect, nature tones her colors by graying them with the dust particles in the atmosphere. Landscape artists imitate nature by glazing their paintings with a muted color, or by adding a little of one color to all the colors for a unifying effect.

A UNIFIED WHOLE

A liberating (but maybe dangerous) realization is that we can use as many colors as we wish, as long as we achieve a unified whole. To observe that a sign has too many colors is inaccurate theoretically. The real problem is that the colors are not unified or that they are incompatible.

To unify bulletin colors, you add a little of the dominant color (often a background color) to the subordinate colors. I saw a sign recently that had attractive and workable colors, but that didn't come off as well as it could have. It was a 2' x 3' sign with a dark brown background, white lettering and a lime-yellow 2" border . . . attractive colors, but a mediocre sign. The lime-yellow border totally overpowered the white lettering. The solution would have been to add a little of the brown background color to the lime-yellow border to tone it down and unify it with the background. This sign was an example of what frequently goes wrong for sign designers who like to use a lot of color. Their selection of colors is good, but the sign ends up looking spotty because they're not unified. Generally, you should unify middleground and background colors, leaving the foreground color pure or clean.

Master painters and designers have long recognized that beauty is the natural product of good order and good proportions. Our work as sign painters is subject to the same causal relationship. For me, the term "good" as used in design means "stability and believability." For example, imagine the shapes of Figure 56 to be building blocks. The bottom black block looks the strongest and thus, capable of supporting the other blocks. If we turned Figure 56 upside-down it would look top heavy, but we would still see a relationship between the blocks because of the rhythm of their shape and orderly gradation of value. If we scrambled the order of the blocks this figure would look chaotic and lose all design appeal.

To ensure consistency in my work, I use what I call the "1-2-3" of design: Foreground, middleground and background — bold, medium and light — dark, middle and light tonal values. Graphics look more interesting, better balanced and not as contrived when broken into three unequal parts. One-two-three can also apply to color and its tonal value, line value (which includes lettering, illustration and ornamentation) and copy blocks.

CONTRAST

Poor *contrast* in value (lights and darks) is the most common error in the use of color. It's important to teach the imaginative child within us the difference between "bright" colors and "contrasting" colors. For example, imagine two

Figure 56 Distinct contrast in color values is preferred for production purposes.

lines of lettering, in a lightface Helvetica about one inch tall on a white background. The top line is lettered in fire red, and the second line is lettered in brilliant blue. Chances are the creative child will think the red lettering is stronger and will show up better than the blue, but in reality it will not. The blue lettering is twice as dark in its contrast with white as the fire red. Use the color/value wheel in Figure 55 to better understand the relative value of light and dark in bulletin paints.

The effectiveness or strength of a color is contextual. That is to say, it's always modified to a greater or lesser extent by its association with another color (or colors) and their respective masses. In the previous example of equal proportions of fire red and brilliant blue, we saw that the blue dominated the red. To reverse the effect (that is, to have the red dominate the blue), we would have to increase the size and mass of the fire red lettering to an approximately four-inch-high bold stroke. This larger mass of red next to the lightface blue letters causes a new optical effect. It gives a new significance to the white negative space around the blue letters, causing the brilliant blue to gray a little, thus reducing its contrast with the white background. The exact opposite has happened with the new mass of red. There is no substitute for time and experience in becoming sensitive to the changes that occur with color as the proportional relationships change.

AN ONGOING CHALLENGE

Realistically, we rarely have the opportunity to test our full knowledge or capabilities with color. This shouldn't be disappointing though, because we have an equally interesting and ongoing challenge in the art of layout — how to use creatively the more-or-less standard colors of our daily routine. By creative use, I don't mean discovering some new combination of colors; I mean laying out a sign that looks so right that red and black on white looks fantastic. Graphic expression and personality are more a matter of line, mass and spatial relationships than of color. Some of the most colorful signs ever seen are in black and white!

A clean, modern look comes from simplicity. If you are doing a lot of knock-out work with heavy copy, a good technique is to use only one strong contrasting color for headings (where fairly neat lettering is required), and then to use a tint, or a low contrasting color on secondary copy. The low contrast

Fig. 57

Fig. 58

in the secondary copy will conceal little flaws in letter construction, enabling you to letter it as quickly as possible. The overall believability will have been established in the layout and strong, crisp lettering in the heading. I use this approach in just about all signs.

Figure 56 represents the value range I always try to work with. For production purposes I choose a background color that is definitely dark or definitely light. Dark is any color that is at least 50% or more on the value wheel, and light is 10% or less. I do this because the values between dark and light require too much tampering with to strike a clear contrast. If the top box in Figure 56 represented a light background, I would use the remaining three values for the lettering. If the bottom box in Figure 56 represented a dark background, I would use the first three values for the lettering.

Figures 57 and 58 are for your experimentation. What colors would you use? First take a traditional approach — use whatever your imagination comes up with. Then try something new, using the color wheel as a guide. See what you can do with a triad of colors, or a split complement. Don't hesitate to tint or shade your colors if you think it will help. Figure 57 is a sandblasted sign, with real bamboo at the bottom.

Figure 57   Trace this sketch and render it in color, using the color wheel as a guide.

Figure 58   Trace this sketch and render it in color, using the color wheel as a guide.

Color is a lot of fun. It has universal appeal, bringing life to an otherwise in-animate object, a sign. To further your understanding of color, I suggest that you try oil painting (if you haven't already). You can gain more experience in, and understanding of color in the first few months of landscape painting than you can in years of commercial sign painting.

9

"Super Graphics are dramatic and forceful; they demand attention."

Super Graphics

The term "Super Graphic" is used loosely by most artists, and means different things to different people. It is most often defined as a modern, bigger-than-life design, featuring either a pictorial, an abstract design, lettering or a combination thereof.

For our purposes, a *Super Graphic* is a visual effect, not a thing or a product. It is the design alternative to natural layout, which is the harmonious subordination of the composition to the format. A Super Graphic visually overpowers the format, causing the format to be of little or no design significance. It is a visually independent design or layout that is complete in and of itself. This concept applies equally to sub-formats, as described in chapter 2.

Super Graphic is a modern term for a phenomenon or essence that has always existed in graphics. Theatrical showcards (in years gone by) often were rendered as Super Graphics, only no one called them that. Instead, these showcards or signs were said to be "punchy," or to have a lot of impact. It is amazing how an idea can catch on once it's given an appealing name.

Super Graphics are dramatic and forceful; they demand attention. It is important not to confuse this term with the term "graphics," as in "wall graphics." A wall graphic can be designed or conceptualized either as a natural layout or as a Super Graphic.

Both natural and Super Graphic layouts have two compositional variants or choices — *formal* or *informal*. Thus far, we have discussed formal layout only. Informal layout will be discussed in the next chapter.

TRITE GRAPHICS

Figures 59 and 60 are examples of a Super Graphic approach we might use as sign painters. Figure 59 qualifies as a Super Graphic, but is not as interesting or as effective as Figure 60. Figure 59 is emotionally trite; this type of design is overused, commonplace, and boring. Every sign does not have to be an original idea, but every old idea should be made to look fresh and interesting. Your success as an artist is more dependent on how people *feel* (their emotional response) about your signs than what they think.

The idea of fresh and interesting graphics refers to the way the different elements are prioritized and distinguished. If it weren't for the fact that "Cycle Shop" has a deep drop shadow, the monotonous line value in this sketch would be more obvious, and the overall effect consequently weaker. Note that Figure 59 is almost all foreground, except for the word "Entrance."

The reversed panel at the bottom of both Figures 59 and 60 are sub-formats. The lettering in the sub-format in Figure 59 isn't "natural" or "Super Graphic" in effect; it is conflicting. Notice how the arrow looks okay, but the lettering doesn't. Why? Due to its line value and spatial relationships, the arrow in Figure 59 is Super Graphic in effect. The weight of the stroke in "Entrance" should be a little bolder, so that it contributes to this effect.

Another problem in Figure 59 is the proportional relationship between "Bob's" and "Cycle Shop"; they almost divide the white panel in half. Notice

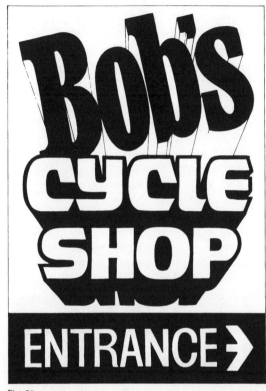

Fig. 59

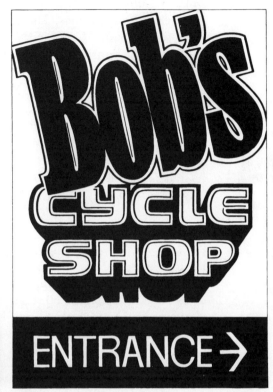

Fig. 60

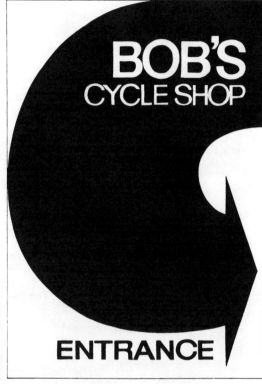

Fig. 61

that "Bob's" and "Cycle Shop" are not only very close in line value, but that the silhouettes created by each are equal in height and volume. A real no-no! Nothing in nature is equal. Look around the room you're in — nothing appears to be the same size, except duplicates at the same distance. Besides the use of color, a sense of space — foreground, middleground and background — is one of the most powerful ways of appealing to the emotions of your audience. Please reread chapter 8 on the use of color, especially the part about the way the mind processes information.

Notice the obvious foreground, middleground and background in Figure 60, and that the copy is definitely prioritized. The point could be argued that the word "Bob's" is too large. If "Cycle Shop" is more important, it should be the largest element on the sign. In my opinion it could go either way, depending

Figure 59   A Super Graphic overpowers the format.

Figure 60   Note the definite sense of foregound, middleground, and background.

Figure 61   A Super Graphic that uses a symbol (the arrow) as its dominant element.

Figure 62 Illustrations can be very effective as Super Graphics.

on circumstances. With this type of sign, the more traditional approach would be to emphasize the product, but . . . is that what is really best for the client?

READING THOUGHT GROUPS

People like to deal with people, not corporations, companies, stores or bicycle shops. In the case of Figure 60, we fulfill that desire by emphasizing "Bob's." Take a quick glance at Figure 60. What does it say? Very few, if any, would read "Bob's," "Cycle Shop," "Entrance." The brain tries to make as much sense as possible out of what it sees. Figure 60 would read conceptually and graphically as a single thought. To just read it as "Bob's" is similar to an incomplete sentence for the brain.

The problem in the sign business is that we continue to edit and interpret copy traditionally. We assume all important copy has to be big, or it will not be read. This assumption is one of the chief roadblocks to improving one's design skills. Perhaps a good comparison is music. How interesting or appealing would a song be if it had only one note, and was played at the same volume all the way through?

Figure 61 is a Super Graphic that uses a symbol, the arrow, as its dominant element. This sketch directs traffic first, then identifies "Bob's." This is probably closer to what most artists would consider to be a Super Graphic. You see and feel the power of the arrow and its obvious emotion, with little awareness of the format.

There is an interesting design fault in Figure 61. The top right-hand side of the format is competing with the arrowhead. Do you see how the top right-hand corner almost forms an arrowhead on its own? This effect results from the black negative space being framed by the imaginary line at the top of "Bob's" and the top edge of the format. Note that the edge of the format to the right of "Bob's" is not nearly as strong as the edge of the format above "Bob's." How would you eliminate the competition between the "real" arrowhead and the top right-hand corner?

The clip-art puppies in Figure 62 are another example of Super Graphics. They dominate the top of the format, while the lettering is subordinate. Overlapping an illustration on the edge of a circle like this is very effective. It contributes to the bigger-than-life appeal of Super Graphics.

When you break the edge of a format with your design as in Figure 62, it must be done with enough power and gusto so it doesn't conflict with the edge of the format. Note that the illustration of the puppies leads the eye towards the optical center of the sign. Whenever you break the edge of the format like this, it's important not to rhythmically lead the eye out of the composition.

ILLUSTRATIONS

Let's change the subject for a moment, and talk briefly about the use of illustrations and cartoons on signs. They are very popular with the average sign buyer. A good cartoon or illustration communicates directly, involving the viewer on an emotional level. For layout purposes, they should be thought of and handled just like blocks of copy. It is not unusual to see a sign with good artwork (an illustration or cartoon) compromised by bad layout. It should dominate, or be subordinate to the main copy.

Lettering over artwork can be effective when handled well; the problem is, it usually isn't. More often than not, the lettering and illustration conflict. The secret lies in having a definite background/foreground relationship between the two, which requires an expert sensitivity to tonal and line values. I am sure we have all tried lettering over artwork, only to wish we hadn't. An important point to keep in mind about cartoons and illustrations is that a sense of space and believability are far more important than the exactness of your drawing.

Figure 63 didn't work the way I had hoped it would. It has three distinct areas of design that are not integrated as a whole. Each one may be considered a Super Graphic, illustrating its independent graphic power. The top reversed panel is an interesting example in that its power and impact is in the negative space instead of the lettering.

The star in Figure 63 appears almost three-dimensional. The interesting thing about this star is that it is formed by the negative space of the arrowheads. The shape of the negative space is easily identified in this case, because it forms a "known" thing — a star. The next time you hear someone say "Negative space is just a fancy word for blank space," you may want to draw them a star made of arrowheads. Just because we haven't seen or experienced something personally, doesn't mean it doesn't exist or isn't possible.

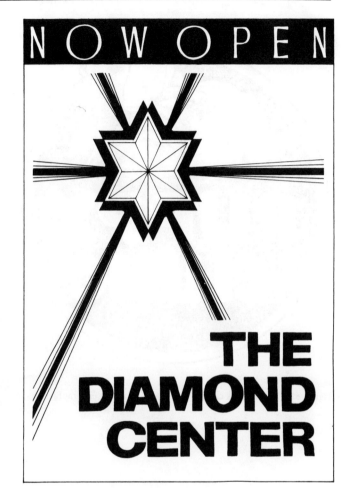

Figure 63   Notice the optical illusion created by the arrow heads.

The bottom lettering of Figure 63, "The Diamond Center" is an informal Super Graphic. It is not as dynamic as the previous examples, but it still dominates and overpowers the format. The top reversed panel of Figure 63 is a formal Super Graphic. Do you see the difference? Formal is any composition or shape that is centered on a vertical axis, either its own or that of the format. Informal is in the eye of the beholder.

"...like attracts like."

Informal Layout

The term "informal" may apply to either the overall layout or a part of the composition, such as a single copy block. A sign may have a formal layout with some informal parts or it may have an informal layout with formal parts. A sign may be entirely informal, both in its parts and in the whole composition.

In general, *informal layout* means that individual parts or silhouettes as well as their placement within the format are more casual or irregular in appearance than those in formal layout. Successful informal layout requires a keen sensitivity to symmetry (see chapter 2) and compulsive graphic relativity (see glossary).

The term informal layout can be misleading. For some it may suggest a style or look that is without discipline, order or reason. Nothing could be farther from the truth. As with all good art, you just don't see the principle at work behind it.

A LITTLE EXTRA CHARACTER

All design elements are either visually independent, or they relate graphically to another design element, as in compulsive graphic relativity. The relationship may be of letter to letter (as in a word), sentence to sentence, silhouette to silhouette, rhythm to rhythm, line value to line value, or color to color. Awareness of these relationships is fundamental to seeing and designing. It has a particular importance in informal composition due to the casual and irregular silhouettes that are frequently created. Irregular shapes are like casual or italic lettering in that they require extra air space around them so they aren't conflicting visually with another element.

It might be fun to use informal composition at every opportunity for a while. Sometimes it's the easiest solution, as in Figure 66. At other times it can be a "mind bender" and time consuming, requiring delicate decisions of balance.

Figure 64 is a combination of informal and formal silhouettes. This layout was not spontaneous or easy for me. It represents more design time than could be considered practical. It contains four different alphabets and a couple of dangerous tricks. The tricks are what really created all the problems. The word "Informal" was double-spaced and laid out at the top edge to give the format more of a role in the overall design. It gives an otherwise uninteresting format a little extra character. Compare the formats of Figures 64, 65 and 66. Note that Figure 64's format suggests a certain image and has an emotional quality that neither Figure 65 or 66 has. It's important also to notice that Figure 64's format has remained subordinate to the main message.

The informal silhouette of "Sign Design" in Figure 64 and its exaggerated interior shape work fairly well. The only problem is that it's compromised by the "L" in the word "Layout." The "L" is too bold and/or too close to the bottom loop of the "g" in the word "Design," creating visual conflict. If this relationship of the "L" and "g" is bad, then why isn't the relationship of the "o" and the bottom loop of the "g" bad as well? They are not visually conflicting, but what is the reason in terms of compulsive graphic relativity?

Fig. 64

Fig. 65

Fig. 66

The goal is to know in advance or be able to predict whether a design is going to work or not. An understanding of compulsive graphic relativity would tell you that because of the line value and proximity of the second stroke in the "L," it relates graphically more to the bottom loop of the "g" than it does to the first stroke of its own letter. The "o" and the "g" do not conflict to the point of distraction because of the contrasting line value and because the rhythm of the two bold strokes in the "o" is just strong enough to maintain the integrity of the letter. In addition, the interior negative space of the "g" provides a nice clean field for the top of the "o."

LIKE ATTRACTS LIKE

It may be said that in signage "Like attracts like," depending on the amount of air space between them. Bold line value relates to bold, light line value relates to light, imaginary or theoretical lines relate to their counterparts.

Figure 64 Informal and formal silhouettes arranged to create an informal composition.

Figure 65 Think of, and arrange illustrations as though they are blocks of copy.

Figure 66 A margin-flush-left layout is particularly advantageous when you are faced with heavy copy — no worries about keeping the copy centered. You can devote your full attention to letter forms and speed.

Figure 65 has a compositional pattern very similar to Figure 64. The line value in the clip-art illustration of the dancers is too light, but adequate to demonstrate that illustrations should be thought of and arranged just like blocks of copy. Note the effect of contrast between the informal silhouette of the dancers and the regimented, formal block of copy. Note also the strong reinforcement of the vertical axis, which assists in creating a feeling of drama and excitement.

The design of Figure 66 is one of the simplest and most profitable approaches to take in sign layout. Whoever invented this type of composition belongs in the "Designer Hall of Fame" (if there is one). A margin flush left layout is particularly advantageous when faced with heavy copy . . . no worries about keeping the copy centered. You can devote your full attention to letter form and speed! Notice in Figure 66 how the imaginary lines at the left, and at the bottom of the silhouette of copy relate to the edges of the format, involving it quietly in the overall design. The arrow is acting as a counter-weight to the copy, yet it is visually independent, not relating to any other element. An arrow requires enough space to fully express its direction and rhythm. If the arrow was too close to one of the margins, it would not only create visual conflict between itself and the margin, but would also cause the diagonal corners to become competitive and conflicting.

Figure 67 has a traditional, industrial look. It is a formal composition with a few informal parts. The "10" is almost a Super Graphic, but not quite. Color could do wonders for this black-and-white sign. As it is now, there is too much equality in the proportional relationships. It's just line after line of copy, with boring silhouettes. Note also the repetitive and equal areas of negative space.

Use a white piece of paper or your imagination to cover all the copy in Figure 67 except "10 Acres." This much of the sign looks good; it has drama and interesting contrast in line value. The demi-bold roman italic lettering looks snappy against the condensed lettering in the "10." Now lower your paper and let "Will Build to Suit" come into view. Notice how this block of copy doesn't have the personality that "10 Acres" does. "Will Build to Suit" would be more interesting to the eye if it were lettered in lightface, or reduced in height a little and made a bold stroke. Either approach would be an improvement. Note the equal areas of negative space that now exist in this top section

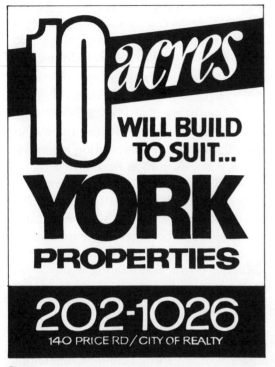

Fig. 67

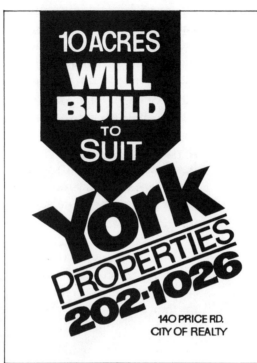

Fig. 68

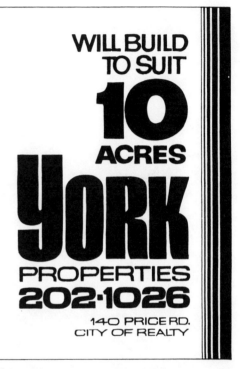

Fig. 69

of the sign. The visual effect of changing the line value of "Will Build to Suit" to a light line would be to gray the lettering and allow more negative space in this area. If it had been lettered in a bold stroke, the lettering and silhouette of the copy block would have become more important as a design element. Also, it would have rhythmically played well with the reversed panel of "Acres," thereby reducing the visual strength and boredom of the negative space in that area.

Cover the top part of Figure 67 with your paper and look at the rest of the layout from "York" down. This part of the sign looks good; it is clean in appearance and has interesting contrast of line value.

Which sign is easier to look at — Figure 67 or Figure 68? Is negative space wasted in Figure 68? Is the clarity and shape of the silhouettes important? Does the line value play a role in leading the eye through the composition?

Figure 67 A formal composition with informal parts.

Figure 68 An informal composition with formal parts.

Figure 69 Give the eye a clear, prioritized choice.

Figure 68 is an informal composition with formal copy blocks. Emphasis was put on "Will Build" for two reasons. The first was to protect the integrity of the reversed panel it is sitting in. Conceptually, this meant doing a subordinate natural layout within the panel. The dominant design of this sign is the relationship and mass of the reversed panel against the "York Properties" block of copy. The goal was to not do anything that would compete or distract from the basic shapes. The second reason for emphasizing "Will Build" instead of "10 Acres" was for the purpose of rhythm in line value. Note the rhythm of "Will Build," "York" and the phone number. If "10 Acres" had been lettered in a bold stroke at the top, it would have distorted the shape of the reversed panel and would have rhythmically related to the top edge of the format. A possible alternative would have been to letter "Will Build to Suit" small at the top, and emphasize the "10" in the optical center of the panel.

THINK ARCHITECTURALLY

Did you notice Figure 68 has only one alphabet? The basic design creates the image; there was no need to use any other alphabets. A common mistake many sign painters make is to "creatively" change alphabets, thinking they're making a sign more interesting or effective. Although in chapter 7 it was said (with discretion) that we could use as many alphabets as necessary, the rule of thumb is design function, not creative impulse. When relating blocks or silhouettes of copy, it is better to think like an architect or a structural engineer than like an abstract artist.

The rules and principles of design are many, but few are hard and fast. All terms and definitions are contextual . . . which leaves us as designers in the position of continuously re-interpreting the criteria. It is seldom spoken of in the sign industry, but the reality is that a mature artist is as much a philosopher as a technician. You will not become a great sign painter just by painting signs or reading about them. It's the totality of your emotional, psychological, social and educational experience, and the integrated awareness thereof, that will be self-actualizing.

Figure 69 looks mechanical. What would you do to make this sign more appealing? I see two things I would like to change. The first would be to make the word "Acres" slightly bolder and taller. Note the negative space under and to the right of the word "Acres." Does it bother you? Why? It compromises the parallel rhythms of the vertical stripes and the rhythm of the imaginary straight line at the right-hand margin of the copy, causing the copy to break into two different blocks. The design would be stronger and clearer if the copy formed one continuous, imaginary straight line on the right-hand side.

The second change I propose in Figure 69 would be to make the line value of the word "Properties" lighter. As it is now, it competes with the phone number. If the phone number looked stronger, it would then rhythmically relate to "York" and "10 Acres," and would lead the eye through the composition in a more positive way. Always give the eye a clear, prioritized choice.

Troubleshooting Your Layout

In this chapter, we will summarize the principles we have covered in this book and provide a systematic method you can use to troubleshoot *your* layouts. If you are dissatisfied with a particular sketch or sign that you have just finished, and are not sure why, refer to this chapter, and analyze your composition with these "guideposts" of sign design.

We must remain both intellectually and emotionally alive — have enough spontaneity to seize upon a creative revelation, while at the same time, have the courage and humility to correct ourselves. In the final analysis, we all end up self-taught. Self-correction is the beginning of self-actualization. Until then, very little happens. A teacher can only *describe* things to us. The student, in a sense, *rediscovers* them, and breathes new life into them. These "things" are not ends or absolutes — they are beginnings. They are the abstract elements of art that are named and defined for the purpose of communication. Use theory as a basis for self-correction and as a launching pad for creativity.

Be patient with yourself as you critique your work. Learning to "see" cause and effect takes time, as well as a variety of experiences. All artists go through the same learning process: just as soon as we think we've "got it," we are humbled by a new level of awareness.

As you analyze your layout, keep in mind that you want to read it graphically, not culturally. Example: Imagine the word "Signs" spelled correctly, but spaced poorly. The spelling is culturally right, but the spacing is graphically wrong. Bad letter spacing simply forms irregular or awkward patterns of positive and negative spaces. The same observation may be made about all bad layout. Awkward or irregular patterns create ambiguous graphic relationships. Good design is composed of clear, concise relationships.

Use the following checklist to analyze your completed signs or sketches. Do not use it to plan or design with. During the conceptual phase, too many rules can inhibit your creativity. You will notice that some of the questions are repeated, only in different contexts. As you pass through one door of knowledge, you face another, all the while seeing and understanding more and finding deeper meaning in the original questions.

Some sections in this outline will not apply to your particular sign. For example, if you have composed a natural layout, then the questions under "Super Graphic" will not be of benefit. The questions are organized to lead you through your composition checkpoint by checkpoint. Take your time and study your sign carefully. Any trouble spots and their solutions will be revealed with the aid of this list.

Refer to the glossary of terms frequently as a refresher and as food for thought. Pay particular attention to the definition of symmetry. It is the ultimate goal in all graphics. Remember also that our signs are a part of a shared environment. What we do visually impacts on our community. Respect it, and it will respect you.

TROUBLESHOOTING CHECKLIST

I. THE GRAPHIC ESSENCE

A. First Impressions

1. Is the first impression of the sign good?

2. Does it have eye and emotional appeal?

3. Is the overall composition unified?

4. Is the eye drawn quickly to the most important copy?

5. Then, is the eye led through the copy in the order of priority?

B. Hot Spots

1. Are there any "hot spots" or areas of immediate visual conflict?

2. Does the negative space compete with the lettering anywhere in the sign?

3. Do the individual lines of copy relate well to each other, or are they competing?

4. Are any parts drawing the eye to the border of the sign before drawing it to the next word or line?

C. Appropriate Image

1. Does the sign convey the appropriate image for the subject?

2. Are the letter styles appropriate?

3. Are the colors appropriate?

II. LAYOUT

A. Copy Interpretation

1. Is the copy interpreted correctly, with the proper importance assigned to each idea?

2. In the interpretation and prioritizing of the copy, were the thoughts well separated into idea groups that lay out nicely and facilitate organizing the composition?

3. Is the line value assigned to the copy consistent with the priority of thought?

4. Were opportunities taken to rearrange the order of the copy to facilitate layout or to achieve a more desirable effect?

5. Should any words be deleted, abbreviated, or added in order to create more pleasing silhouettes?

6. Is the copy organized and prioritized so that it creates a main focal point for the eye to be drawn to immediately?

7. Is the main copy anchored in or near the optical center?

8. Is the eye then led through the layout consistent with the priority of thought?

B. Compulsive Graphic Relativity

1. Are there any areas of visual conflict?

2. Is the conflict caused by inconsistent or competing rhythms of line value, color or spacing?

3. Does the background (negative space) visually compete anywhere with the lettering (positive space)?

4. Is there enough air space in the margins?

5. Are any parts drawing the eye to the border of the sign before drawing it to the next word or line of copy?

6. Is there proper space between words, lines, and blocks of copy so that they remain separate, yet still relate visually and read through well?

C. Natural Layout/Super Graphic

1. *Natural Layout*
   a. If the composition is informal, does the copy maintain a well-balanced, unified whole?
   b. If the composition is formal, is the overall silhouette rhythmically consistent with the dominant axis of the format?
   c. Is the main copy anchored in the optical center?
   d. Is the layout symmetrical?
   e. Are any of the elements alarming to the eye, such as having too little or too much of an angle in the lines of copy or shapes of the silhouettes?
   f. Do the rhythms of any of the individual elements conflict with the format or the dominant axis?
   g. Are sub-formats well integrated with the whole, and do they conform to the same theoretical principles that apply to the major format?
   h. Is the design architecturally sound?

2. *Super Graphic*
   a. If the layout was meant to be a Super Graphic, does it clearly overpower the format, and create a visually independent design?

b. Is the Super Graphic dramatic and forceful, or is it too weak, causing conflict with the format?

c. Does it have a pleasing silhouette?

d. If part of the sign is a Super Graphic, but the rest is subordinate to the format, has care been taken to unify the whole?

e. Is the design architecturally sound?

D. Silhouettes

1. Does the overall arrangement of the layout create a pleasing silhouette?

2. Do the individual copy blocks form their own pleasing silhouettes that relate well and flow with each other?

3. Are there any alarming or radical indentations that cause a silhouette to conflict with its dominant rhythm?

E. Line Value

1. Has a definite sense of foreground, middleground, and background been created through the use of varying line value (light, medium, and bold)?

2. Is the line value consistent with the priority of the copy, and does it lead the eye through the composition?

3. Did you consider changing line value, as opposed to changing color, to add interest?

4. Is the layout compromised by demi-relationships of line value?

5. Are the individual lines and their line value so arranged that they play well off each other and create eye appeal by the placement of light against dark and vice versa?

6. Has using contrasting line value within sub-formats been considered, to create focal points wherever appropriate?

F. Rhythms

1. Are the rhythms of the various elements harmonious throughout the sign?

2. Check the following for harmonious rhythms:

a. The relationship between the format and the main silhouette.

b. The integration of sub-silhouettes to the main silhouette.

c. The patterns of positive and negative spaces.

d. Light, medium, and bold line values.

e. The recurring patterns of color.

3. Do the dominant rhythms reinforce the development of the message?

4. Are any of the rhythms monotonous or corny?

III. LETTERING

A. Letter Styles

1. Is the image the alphabets communicate appropriate to the subject, and are they really legible?

2. Do the alphabets work well with each other, or is there visual conflict and competition between them?

3. Is there a basic flaw in the original design of the alphabet that makes it difficult to create pleasing rhythms and silhouettes?

4. Is there conflict caused by competing rhythms or by poor spacing (graphic punctuation)?

5. Is there appropriate use of, and clear distinction between display alphabets and text alphabets?

6. Are any of the letter styles too tricky, elaborate, or time consuming?

7. If the alphabet is improvised, are the individual letters conceptually composed around a vertical and horizontal axis in a pleasing manner?

8. If you are using an italic or display alphabet with dramatic rhythms, is the air space around it ample enough to eliminate conflict with adjacent elements?

B. Spacing

1. Is the letter and word spacing tight enough to eliminate pockets of negative space that can disrupt the rhythm of a line?

2. Does the space between words in a line of copy keep them separate and distinct yet close enough together that they relate to each other and form a distinct line (horizontal rhythm), before they relate up or down to adjacent copy?

3. Does the space between lines of copy protect their individual rhythms, yet keep them close enough together to form a unified copy block?

4. If the line is an individual thought and not part of a copy block, is the air space separating it from the preceding and succeeding lines enough to keep it distinctly apart, and a unit unto itself?

5. Has care been taken to see that there is more air space in the margins of the sign than between the copy blocks?

6. Does any of the lettering draw the eye to the edge of the format before drawing it to the next line of copy or copy block?

C. Color

1. Is the image the colors convey appropriate to the subject?

2. Is there enough contrast in color value to create pleasing rhythms and eye appeal?

3. Are the dominant colors consistent with the priority of thought?

4. Is color used to lead the eye through the layout?

5. If several colors were used, and they don't work together as well as had been hoped, would adding a little of the background color to one or more unify them or improve their relationship?

6. Are the colors consistent with the idea of foreground, middleground, and background?

LAYOUT CRITIQUES

Study the following layout critiques carefully. Try to "see" each point discussed. The goal is to learn to verbalize what you see. The more specific you can become, the deeper your understanding can grow, and the quicker you can advance.

Figure 70 is a flyer I did for the opening of a friend's new shop. Obviously the prices quoted for banners and truck lettering are ridiculous by today's standards. The original was lettered with showcard paint on an 11" x 17" card. Figure 70 has a certain appeal, which makes it difficult to correct and still maintain the original image. Only after I assigned a definite priority of thought and the appropriate line values to the message did I begin to have reasonable success in revising it.

Your ability in layout is subject to your skill in interpreting and editing copy. Compare Figures 70 and 71, keeping in mind that the eye can't read everything at once. The eye first sees the overall composition, and then starts looking for something of interest.

In a visually competitive situation, Figure 71 would probably be read before Figure 70. Why? Because Figure 71 delivers the most important information first. In revising the layout in Figure 71, I would put less emphasis on the words "Shop" and "Paper," and give more attention to the word "Banner."

My first thought in rendering Figure 71 was to create an overall silhouette with interior shapes and rhythms that were more consistent with the format than they had been in Figure 70. I was conscious of trying to lead the eye to the most important copy in the optical center without drastically changing the image of the original design.

Figure 70 is full of horizontal panels and rhythms that contradict the vertical format. The only reason the layout works is because the overlapping panels which hold the composition together form a silhouette that is vaguely consistent with the format. Compare Figures 70 and 71, and see if your eyes can pick up on these differences.

In Figure 70 "Meet Your New Neighbors" creates a horizontal rhythm, whereas in Figure 71 it creates a vertical rhythm that is consistent with the format. It leads the eye into the composition instead of off the page, as it does in Figure 70.

The "sign panel" in Figure 70 is alarming to the eye and doesn't lead you towards the optical center as it does in Figure 71. The sign panel in Figure 70 is a sub-format, and should have been laid out more in line with its dominant axis. I tried several times in Figure 71 to letter the word "Shop" within the tail of the "g"; however, I just couldn't pull it off. My problem was trying to get the tail of the "g" to reinforce the vertical axis (by making it rounder, instead of elongated), and still letter the word "Shop" within it harmoniously.

I liked the ribbon in Figure 70; however, for the sake of simplicity and clarity, it had to go. From a sales point of view, I felt it would be better not to hide the word "Special" in the ribbon. The stars and bubbles in Figure 71 are excessive and clumsy. They were used to modify a design problem, not for decoration as it may appear. The bottom of the sign panel was too bold and massive looking, and tended to frame the negative space between it and the paper banner copy. The stars and dots were an afterthought used to save the composition. Theoretically, they serve to gray that area, allowing the more important elements to stand out.

The bold line value of "Paper Banners" in Figure 71 serves several purposes:
1. The oval in which it's placed is a sub-format; the bold line value reinforces

Fig. 70

Fig. 71

Figure 70 Compare this sketch with Figure 71.

Figure 71 This sketch has improved rhythms in line value, and the overall silhouette created by the copy is more harmonious with the format than that of Figure 70.

Fig. 72

Fig. 73

Figure 72 Original by Lynn Hollinger .

Figure 73 Revision in line value, and greater margins have improved this sign.

the optical center. 2. The bold lettering plays well against the sign panel, and helps to lead the eye through the composition to the bold telephone number, serving to unify the layout. 3. The bold lettering creates a sense of drama, telling the reader in a very positive way that the price is probably a bargain. The image of these two layouts is what I call "hard core," which just means flashy. From an advertiser's point of view, it is supposed to create a sense of urgency and motivate people to act promptly.

It is a good idea to repeat your company name whenever possible, but not so obviously that it becomes offensive to the reader. Your future depends upon market recognition of your name. The more often you can get people to repeat it, the better; that is, provided that what they say is positive.

I like the dramatic contrast between the name, address and phone number in Figure 71. They flatter each other and make the layout far more interesting to the eye. Notice how the light stroke in the name and address relates back to the itemized list of services. A heavy copy layout like this requires obvious contrasting line values that play back and forth, integrating the entire composition.

Figure 72 is very strong and contemporary looking, like a sign you'd expect a garage to have. Color would greatly enhance this layout.

It's obvious that the signpainter started right by taking the time to assign an order of importance to the copy. Notice how "Auto Service" is anchored in the optical center, a good approach that would have worked a little better if "Sonny Snipe's" wasn't quite so bold. As it is now, "Auto Service" is compromised by the almost equal line value of "Sonny Snipe's."

The silhouette of the first three lines of copy is good. The arrow, which is very strong and equal to the width of "Auto Service," tends to square off the entire layout, creating a bulky appearance. If the arrow was shortened a couple of inches on both ends it would help "Auto Service" stand out and create a smoother overall silhouette. Often a squared silhouette like this becomes too strong a design element and interferes with the immediate legibility of the copy.

To demonstrate the power of adequate space in the margins, imagine this composition just as it is — with one exception. Add about 20% more air space all the way around it. Greater air space in the margins would eliminate many of the problems this sign now has.

Due to the lack of negative space in the margins, the overall silhouette is not as well defined as is some of the air space within the layout. In particular, notice the negative space around and between the "o" and the "S" in "Auto Service," and between the arrow up to and throughout the word "Center." These pockets of negative space are framed by the lettering and are competing with it for attention. They would not be nearly as noticeable had there been more negative space in the margin.

Figure 73 has many of the same problems that Figure 72 has, but they're not quite as noticeable due to the revisions in line value and adequate margins. Perfection of spatial relationships is rarely achieved, but it remains the ultimate goal. As commercial artists, our role is to create an orderly and visually stimulating first impression within a reasonable amount of time.

Keep in mind that an arrow has a very strong motion about it and, if not given adequate margins, can conflict with other elements. All letters, symbols or lines that suggest or create action require more "breathing room" (negative space).

The colors on the truck in Figure 74 are: light blue in the key, light rust-orange in the lock face and olive green in the safe; all are outlined in black. "Baker's Locksmith Service" and the phone number are lettered in black. The itemized services to the lower right are lettered in gray with red bullets. The bands above and below the phone number are a deep rust color.

I will discuss Figure 74 first as it stands without the major revisions that are suggested in Figure 75. The idea is to learn to "see" and understand why a sign looks the way it does. What is the magic of superior graphic expression? What can we know in advance of making a layout that will help us to not make the same mistakes over and over again? Plenty! In fact, many artists already possess enough knowledge of the particulars — they just don't see how they apply to the whole picture.

The pictorial symbols in Figure 74 illustrate an awareness of the need for unity which has not been fully integrated conceptually. Notice how the key, lock face and safe are overlapping and tied together with the bold outline. They look strong and are held together as a unit. Had they been illustrated as separate units (not overlapping), they would look weak and probably compete with each other. Imagine the key, lock and safe to be letters that form a word or a thought group. Now imagine the words "Baker's Locksmith Ser-

Fig. 74

Fig. 75

Figure 74 Original by Raymond Chapman.

Figure 75 Prioritizing and interpreting copy is essential to successful layout.

Figure 76   Original by Lane Walker.

vice" to be pictorial symbols (just like the key, lock and safe), and that you want them to look strong and unified also. Artists are taught to unify a composition when working pictorially. They think in terms of masses and how they relate. Yet sign painters don't make the same connection in lettering. They don't see the mass or silhouettes of words and thought groups, and their relationship to the format.

The pictorial symbols and the phone number in Figure 74 are good, strong elements in this layout. The design begins to weaken with "Baker's Locksmith Service." Notice that it doesn't have the strength or unity that the pictorial or phone number does. A great improvement would be made if all the lettering was tighter. This could best be accomplished by enlarging and elongating the lettering in each line, therefore enhancing the horizontal rhythm. Notice how the vertical thrust or rhythm of each letter in "Locksmith" is conflicting with the dominant horizontal rhythm of the overall design. Tighter letter spacing would have produced more emphasis on the imaginary straight line at the top and bottom of the lettering, which would then reinforce the horizontal feeling.

In Figure 75 I have re-interpreted the copy and simplified the composition. Please use your imagination to insert the colors within the pictorial symbols. I would leave the phone number as it is in Figure 74. The pictorial of the key, lock and safe identify the service quite well, making it possible to give more attention to the client's name. The name "Baker's" is also shorter, and has more harmonious shapes than the awkward combination of letters found in "Locksmith."

Figure 75 offers two good examples of the effect of rhythm on layout that may be easily understood when compared to Figure 74. The first example demonstrates recurring rhythm and its power to unify a composition. In Figure 74 the pictorial symbols are very bold; their strength is not reflected anywhere else in the layout. They may be viewed as an independent design element. In Figure 75 "Baker's" works as a recurring rhythm of the pictorial symbols, due to its bold line value. The second example is the strong horizontal rhythm found in the words "Locksmith Service" in Figure 75. Compare the negative space around the "L" of "Locksmith" in both figures. In Figure 74 the "L" seems more visually isolated; it relates equally to the safe, "B," "o" and the word "Service." The negative space between the "L" and "o" in Figure 75 is not nearly so bothersome, due to the strong horizontal rhythm and recurring rhythm of line value found in Microgramma lettering.

Figure 76 is a sketch of a showcard done with a felt tip pen. The original was 3¾" x 6." My sketch (Figure 77) was lettered in showcard paint, 5¾" x 9¼". In Figure 76, the artist's intention was to have the slash under the word "Congratulations" to appear gray, not solid as it is now.

The first impression of Figure 76 is good and strong, especially in view of the fact that this is one of the most awkward combinations of words a sign painter can be plagued with in a vertical format. The use of a condensed alphabet for the main copy, and its placement in the optical center is harmonious with the rhythm of the format. The main copy's visual impact and mass give this card an immediate professional feel.

Notice how the words "Anniversary Celebration Sweepstakes Winners" individually form horizontal shapes and rhythms, but as a group they form a vertical copy block that is consistent with the format. This is a nice way of stimulating the eye with a subtle conflict of rhythms, as opposed to using tricky embellishments such as stars, etc.

The word "Congratulations" is important in this copy, and needs to be prominent. The problem, though, was how to lay it out without creating a monotonous silhouette when viewed in relationship to "Anniversary Celebration." It was also important that "Congratulations" be either harmonious, subordinate or overpowering to the format. As it is now it relates to the rest of the copy only because of the recurring bold line value in the script and the bold stroke of "Anniversary," etc. The word "Congratulations" doesn't work quite as well as it should because the silhouette of the word and its consequent rhythm flow to either the left- or right-hand margin before they relate downward through the composition. An alternative for "Congratulations" might have been to letter it upper and lower case, in the same alphabet as "Anniversary" (medium stroke), with the same spacing between it and "Anniversary," etc. (More about this later.)

The copy block at the bottom of Figure 76 forms a horizontal silhouette. Notice how the theoretical or imaginary straight line at the bottom of "At Registration Desk" frames the air space between itself and the inset line. This relationship reinforces the horizontal rhythm, which contradicts the vertical format. Note that, even though the copy block is physically closer to the preceding copy, it graphically relates to the bottom of the sign.

Figure 77 Always check and double-check your interpretation of the copy.

It would have been easier to resolve this problem if the word "Merchandise" could have been eliminated. The silhouette of this bottom block of copy needed to be a little softer and more consistent with the vertical format. (See the shape in Figure 77.)

Inset lines and borders are subordinate design elements. They should flatter and reinforce the format. In Figure 76 the inset line at the top and bottom of the sign frames and calls attention to the negative space between it and the border, more than it acts as an accent to the format.

In Figure 77, the goal was to make the sign look a little more festive and easier to read. We discussed earlier the problem with the word "Congratulations" in Figure 76. To better utilize the space available, and to break up the series of long words that had to be read before getting to the punch line "Sweepstakes Winners," I assigned a new priority to the words.

The reversed panel at the top would be a separate card, glued on. "Congratulations" would look and read better if it were elongated and lettered in upper and lower case, instead of all caps. As it is now, the black negative spaces at both sides of the word look awkward and independent of the composition.

Figure 77 offers a lot of food for thought, both good and bad. The bottom copy block is a mess. My goal was to develop a recurring bold line value within this block that would unite it with the rest of the copy. Perhaps the word "Prizes" is too bold, but the silhouette of the copy is fine. (Compare this shape with Figure 76.)

Figure 78 is a framed 14" x 22" real estate sign, lettered in fire red and black. The ampersand ("&") and "MLS" logo are printed in fire red. "Licensed Real Estate Brokers" has a fine red line above and below it. "Branch Office, Shirley Graves, Broker" has a red line under it.

The first impression of the sign is very clean. I like the idea of using the red ampersand between the black "A" and "S." Extra care and consideration needs to be taken when using older style roman letters. They are ornamental and often architecturally weak, making it difficult to develop consistent rhythms. This particular roman alphabet is full of action; each letter looks like it's going someplace (and not necessarily with one of its neighbors). All lines, letters or shapes that suggest movement require extra breathing room.

With a white piece of paper, cover up all the copy in Figure 78 except the

Fig. 78

Fig. 79

word "Agency." Do you see how the word looks much better when given enough air space to express itself? In the first chapter it is mentioned that there are two ways of reading a sign — culturally and graphically. To read a sign graphically is to follow the rhythms and relationship of the shapes (letters or words). Our job is to see to it that the shapes lead the eye through the sign consistent with the order and/or priority of thought. The "A," "&" and "S" in Figure 78 should rhythmically relate to each other before relating to any other element. As they are now, the "A" relates to the "A" in the word "Agency," the ampersand relates to the "en" and the "S" relates to the "y." Figure 78 would have worked much better if the company name had been unified, and a little more contrast and interest had been created in the balance of the copy.

In Figure 79 I took the liberty of changing the style of roman lettering. The open face "A" and "S" and the "MLS" logo are lettered in fire red, with the rest of the copy in black. The inset line represents the frame on the original sign.

The first task was to organize and prioritize the copy. This sign is a little unusual in that it has two logos, two phone numbers, a personal name, license and branch office notices, plus street, city and state. It would have been to

Figure 78 Original by Conrad Johnson.

Figure 79 Form distinct copy blocks that are harmonious with the format.

the customer's advantage to edit some of this copy.

I laid out this sign through a process of elimination. The first step was to organize the "A & S" logo, and find its spot in the composition (knowing it had to be the main focal point). Notice how the bottom of the logo leads your eye to the optical center of the format, and seems to be anchored there. Once the most important copy is successfully laid out, then it simply becomes a matter of not ruining it with the balance of the copy. By this, I mean don't do anything with the rest of the copy that will diminish the cleanliness and strength of the design established by the "A & S" logo. This is where your imagination and ability to interpret copy is really tested. There isn't much room left on the sign, and most of the copy still needs to be laid out.

My next step was to identify the lowest possible point on the sign where the copy could go. The next thing to determine was how close to the logo I could letter without compromising it, and how much space was needed in the left- and right-hand margins. I knew that the left- and right-hand margins should not exceed the width of the "A & S" logo. To do so would be to create a shape or silhouette that would make the sign appear bottom-heavy.

Now we have identified the maximum amount of space and area that is left to letter by process of elimination. The best thing to do is to form one copy block with the remaining words, constructing something that is architecturally sound. The "A & S" logo is "weighty" and needs a good subordinate block under it for support. Note the architectural difference between Figures 78 and 79.

All capital letters were used in the bottom block of Figure 79 to make it easier to unify (taking advantage of the imaginary straight lines at the top and bottom of each line). Notice the shape of the silhouette, and the way the copy was prioritized in height and line value.

The subtleties of design are many, and often contradictory. Describing art is a lot like trying to describe the "shape" of water. We all know it when we see it, but we rarely see or experience it the same way twice.

The first impression of Figure 80 is excellent. It has a lot of impact, yet looks clean and friendly. Hand-lettered flyers are a great way to drum up business. You can mail them to prospective customers, slide them under business doors at night, or leave them with a potential customer after personally introducing yourself.

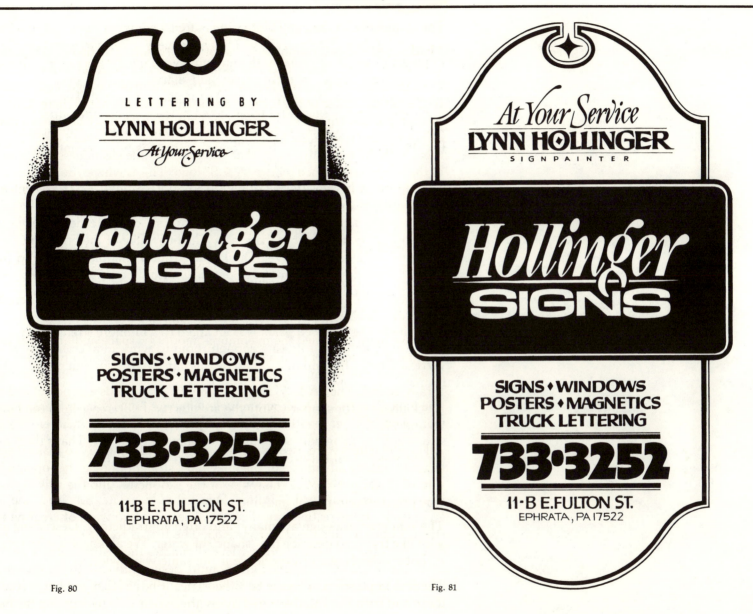

Fig. 80

Fig. 81

Figure 80 Original by Lynn Hollinger.

Figure 81 Examine the subtle differences between Figures 80 and 81.

The silhouettes of the copy blocks in Figure 80 are generally good, but there are more of them than necessary. The challenge is to form as few copy blocks as possible, which also makes design and layout much easier. The silhouette of "Hollinger Signs" is inconsistent and alarming to the eye. Silhouettes should be symmetrical, whether they're formal or informal. The distortion of a silhouette is only successful when taken to the extreme of a Super Graphic. Anything less produces visual conflict. The shape of the negative space under the "H" and in front of the "S" in "Signs" is so strong that it conflicts with the silhouette of "Hollinger Signs."

The line value in the lettering of Figure 80 is interesting, and consistent with the priority of thought. The same care and consideration needs to be taken with borders and ornamentation. They are subordinate design elements; they should be "felt" rather than seen. The line value of the border in Figure 80 is too bold and intrusive. Think background, middleground and fore-ground when designing borders or ornamentation. For example, in Figure 81 the background is the white paper (this page), middleground is the first light line of the border, and foreground is the bold line.

In Figure 81 the reversed panel was enlarged to gain more strength in the op-tical center, and also to create enough room to work in a letter style with a vertical thrust (rhythm) that would tie this panel to the rhythm of the vertical format.

The italic Roman and Microgramma letter styles in "Hollinger Signs" do not work well together in either figure. They both are too soft; neither creates a strong enough imaginary straight line to play off the other. That's the reason for the slash (line) between the two of them in Figure 81.

The 22" x 28" showcard in Figure 82 was a knock-out one-day sale card. To improve this showcard, "Putter Sale" should relate, or lead the eye graphically towards the optical center. There are two ways of creating that effect; both are illustrated in Figure 83. The first is to use upper and lower case letters for the word "Putter." This eliminates the theoretical straight line at the top of the word, thereby giving more design influence to the imaginary line at the bottom. This is the first theoretical rhythm that will begin leading the eye. Note that the second "t" in the word "Putter" in Figure 82 is graphically reaching for the top edge of the format instead of the optical center.

Fig. 82

Fig. 83

Fig. 84

The second way of getting "Putter Sale" to relate more to the optical center is through the use of recurring rhythms in line value. In Figure 83 the line value of "Putter Sale" relates to the price. In Figure 82 it is isolated at the top of the card.

Figure 82 is well-organized, with three distinct copy blocks. The silhouettes of the bottom two blocks are good. The silhouette of "Putter Sale" is too severe. In general, the card would be improved by simply making the price larger and bolder, and by using fewer informal alphabets. Remember that you want contrast. In alphabet choice that means playing informal shapes against formal shapes.

In Figure 84 I used an italic casual and vertical casual (in the golf club brand names). Theoretically the two different casuals visually conflict, and the second one is redundant from a design or image point of view. However, there is always the clock on the wall telling us to get the job done, so for the sake of

Figure 82 Original by Mark Baty.

Figure 83 Use recurring rhythms in line value to unify your composition.

Figure 84 Crisp, clean and fast.

speed it may be necessary to use more casual than we'd prefer. To eliminate the predictable problem of conflicting casual lettering in the brand names in Figure 84, I made them so small, light and tightly grouped that the character of the lettering is of little design significance. The *silhouette* of the brand name copy is the dominant element, which then fits in nicely as a subordinate element of the overall design.

Figures 83 and 84 illustrate the difference between trite layout and good or natural layout. Figure 83 looks stiff and contrived whereas Figure 84 looks like it was born that way. Figure 83 looks graphically like several different ideas, while in Figure 84, the words and the visual effect are one.

Figure 83 has some strange shapes that completely ruin the layout. Do you see them? They are shapes of negative space, all around and within "$25 Ea.," especially the space between the column of brand names and the price. If the brand names were lighter, the negative space would not be so well-defined. This would eliminate the visual discord between the irregular right-hand margin of the brand names' silhouette and the irregular silhouette of the dollar sign and "2."

Interpreting and editing copy to achieve balance without sacrificing the important elements of the message is essential. Note that in Figures 83 and 84, I changed or dropped some of the original wording that was in Figure 82.

Afterword: Always Look Back

I'd like to close this book with a few personal thoughts — observations and experiences that will hopefully comfort, forewarn and yes, inspire! The sign business is a relatively small industry with a poorly recorded history. In years gone by there was a commonality of experience and method. Market conditions and attitudes were similar. You could work in just about any major city, and feel at home as a sign painter. Today, this is no longer the case. Markets and population centers have shifted dramatically. Some parts of the country have literally exploded with new growth and opportunity, while others have remained stagnant, or are, in fact, going backwards, and being abandoned by the talented for greener pastures.

People are attracted to the sign business for many different reasons. I prefer to believe that most newcomers today are motivated by their love for and fascination with the art of hand lettering, just as their predecessors were. It's a beautiful business to be in. It offers both freedom of expression and just financial reward. The only limits are those that are self-imposed. Each generation of sign painters is presented with a new world of opportunities.

We are just like every other group of people — we mirror the attitudes of the community we live in. Those of us that have witnessed success and prosperity think in terms of possibilities. Those that haven't view success as a pipe dream. They argue not only for their own mediocrity, but for that of the industry as a whole. Newcomers to the business should be aware that standards vary tremendously from shop to shop and from state to state. The world is anxiously awaiting our contributions, not our excuses or apologies.

The introduction of mechanical lettering aids and computerized design systems is rapidly changing the economics of the labor market. Many apprentice positions that were once available are now being filled by inexpensive labor at the keyboard of a computer. Aspiring lettering artists must develop their skills to uncommon heights if they are to compete in the market of the future. Computers will replace mediocre sign painters. They are efficient and reliable.

It's ironic, but what many see as the scourge of the sign business — computer graphics — may actually be its salvation. In the right hands, the computer will cut labor costs and improve routine production…freeing the creative mind to concentrate on the more interesting projects. Top lettering and design artists have nothing to fear from the new technologies. In fact, they will profit as never before due to the increased market demand for their exclusive services. Computers are merely instruments of production. It's the operator's ability or inability to lay out well that counts. You've probably heard the saying: "Garbage in — garbage out!" Computers can't make a bad idea or an inappropriate design better — they can only mass produce them with an amazing consistency.

The neatness of computer-generated symbols is admirable, but comparatively of little value. The essence of good sign design isn't the quality of each part (letter, etc.) so much as it is the combination of parts, and how they relate as a whole. This is not a point to pass over lightly. Your future as a lettering artist is dependent upon your ability to demonstrate good design and its value to your employer or client. That is where your true power lies! Don't make the mistake of attempting to compete with computers. Take advantage of their blind spots…develop your aesthetic and business acumen.

I'd like to share a story with you that typifies an attitude (and its consequences) that most of us have encountered as beginners in the sign business. The story has to do with some of the worst advice I've ever received. It was offered to me after completing one of my first wall signs. (Actually, it would be more accurate to say that it was foisted upon me as we were escaping with the loot from a wall job we had just knocked-out.) As we were driving away from the sign I leaned out the passenger's window of the truck. I wanted to see how it looked from a distance. Just as I stuck my head out of the window to see, this older, more experienced painter reached over, whacked me on the shoulder, and said: "Don't ever look back! The customer is satisfied — he's paid us. Our responsibility is to get the job done, get paid for it, and get the ---- out of here. Don't worry about what the sign looks like. The customer can't tell the difference."

This event took place about twenty-four years ago. To make a long story short, while the community tripled in size, this fellow has involuntarily painted fewer and fewer signs over the years. Not because his price isn't right (it has dropped), but because he is running out of customers who "can't tell the difference." It is true that up until the recent past, the image-appropriateness of sign design was secondary to legibility. However, that is no longer the case. The explosion in mass communications has inspired the market greatly, giving it a new awareness and a more dynamic set of visual expectations. There has never been a more opportune time for creative lettering artists.

Always look back, and always look forward — improve your skills and product at every opportunity. You'll not only be protecting your future, but you'll be helping to create a better market for all sign painters. There is a natural phenomenon that takes place in a healthy economy — and that is that the more good sign painters there are, the greater interest and demand there is for the product. In the final analysis we are in this together. Let's keep the lines of communication open and intellectually honest, and the standards high!

Glossary

Axis, Axes   The theoretical central lines around which layouts and letter forms are composed. The axis is used in design to integrate single or multiple graphic elements into a symmetrical whole. There are three axes: vertical, horizontal, and italic. See the illustrated "Natural Layout Formula" in chapter 1 for the placement of axes within the format. In this example the vertical axis is in the mathematical center, and the horizontal axis is located 46% of the way down from the top of the format. Placement of the vertical axis may vary in informal composition. The longest axis is known as the *dominant axis.* The shortest axis is known as the *subordinate axis.*

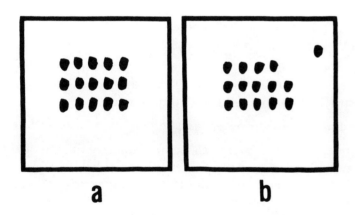

a   b

Compulsive graphic relativity   The phenomenon of a particular design element relating visually to its nearest counterpart or to another design element. Graphic elements are either isolated and visually independent, or they relate to each other and form a group (intentionally or unintentionally). The amount of negative space between elements determines their relationship. Good graphic relationships are consistent with the order of thought, and are pleasing to the eye. Ambiguous graphic relationships are caused by poor spacing.

The illustrations above demonstrate compulsive graphic relativity. Notice in Figure a how the dots relate to each other and form a pattern within the format because they are surrounded by more negative space than exists anywhere within the group. In Figure b, one dot has been removed from the pattern and placed closer to the edge of the format. Notice how it now relates visually to the edge of the format, and no longer appears to be a member of its original design group. That is compulsive graphic relativity. Each design element relates to the nearest dominant design element — whether it be a letter, illustration, decoration, or the edge of the format.

Contrast   Created by using dissimilar or opposing design elements. Clarity in design is achieved by dramatic contrast. Examples include: light against dark, an italic script against a gothic alphabet, warm colors against cool colors.

Due graphic proportion   The correct appropriation of space available versus the relative importance of the copy.

Focal point   The spot or area in a layout that the eye is first attracted to. In natural layout the focal point should lie approximately in the optical center of the format (the intersection of the vertical and horizontal axes).

Formal and informal layout   The two alternatives in natural layout and Super Graphics. Formal is regimented balance; i.e., mathematically equal parts on both sides of an axis. Informal is casual balance; i.e., unequal parts composed around the dominant axis in a visually pleasing manner.

Format   The shape and area of the sign face, or the space to design within. *Sub-formats* may be established by the use of design panels. Sub-formats are subject to the same design principles as the major format.

Graphic essence   The net design effect of single or multiple graphic components; that is, elements viewed individually or as an integrated whole.

Idea group   A segregated block of copy formed by combining similar or related information. A block of copy may be a single subject, as in "Product Features," or be comprised of several bits of information, such as the date, time, and price.

Layout   The organization and arrangement of copy; a stage when proportional relationships of positive and negative spaces are fine-tuned and adapted to a particular format. Think of layout as the *cause* of design, and design as the result or end effect of layout. It is the combination and sum of all applied graphics and their relationship to the format.

Line value   The relative thickness of line in letter strokes, ornamentation, illustration and cartooning. Think in terms of three distinct line values: light, medium, and bold. Use variation in line value as an illustrator would use foreground, middleground, and background. A light line is comparable to background, a medium line is comparable to middleground, and bold is comparable to foreground. The width of the stroke of a lightface letter equals 10% of its height, a medium face letter, 20%, and a boldface letter, 40%. (These percentages do not apply to severely condensed or extended alphabets.)

Natural layout   A composition that is subordinate to the format and is composed around the dominant axis, either formally or informally.

Negative space   The area around and within letter forms, extending out to the edge of the format. It is commonly referred to as the background, white space, or air space.
Note: Negative space is analogous to light. Without light we would be in the dark, unable to see. Without proper negative space, graphic forms become illegible. There is a logical development of proportions of negative space, a sequential hierarchy that is rarely altered. The amount of negative space expands in a consistent manner: letters to words, words to idea groups, idea groups to paragraphs, and paragraphs to format. Thinking of negative space as "graphic punctuation" will help tremendously in achieving clarity and legibility in your design.

Optical center   Located 46% of the way down from the top of the format, at the intersection of the horizontal and vertical axes. All design shapes and forms have two centers: a mathematical center and an optical center. In design, we use the optical center for eye appeal. If the horizontal axis were placed in the mathematical center of the format, visually it would appear to be too low; if placed at the mathematical center of a letter, the letter would appear top heavy.

Positive space   The letter forms and/or any applied graphics. Positive space should rhythmically lead the eye through the composition, consistent with the order and priority of thought.

Reading graphically   Reading the positive and negative spaces and their relationships; reading a composition in terms of its structure as opposed to its cultural sense.

Rhythms   Recurring patterns in line, form or color.

Silhouette   The overall shape or imaginary outline of single or multiple blocks of copy. Ideally, one should create silhouettes that are harmonious and rhythmically consistent with the dominant axis of the format.

Super Graphic   The design alternative to natural layout. A Super Graphic visually overpowers the format, causing it to be of little or no design significance. It is a visually independent design that is complete in and of itself.

Symmetry   The proper or due proportion of the parts and their relationship as a whole; excellence of proportion; when all individual design components are integrated so as to achieve maximum format potential.

Visual conflict   The result of two or more elements in a design simultaneously competing for attention. It is caused by inconsistent or incompatible rhythms of positive and negative spaces. Areas of visual conflict are sometimes referred to as "hot spots."

Index